The Buddha Field

The Chronicles of a Spiritual Adventuress | *Vol. 1*

GISELLE KOY

ISBN: 1479382485
ISBN-13: 9781479382484

ACKNOWLEDGMENTS

I would like to thank the entire "Buddha Field" for this experiment of a modern day mystery school. My love overflows for all of us and the incredible experience we shared.

And of course, I would like to thank all my teachers, both living and ascended.

I would also like to thank Jennifer Hill Robenalt, who helped navigate the murky waters of telling a true story and encouraged me to share it with the world.

DEDICATION

For all initiates of all times

TABLE OF CONTENTS

PREFACE

The first thing I was taught by a spiritual master was:

Be careful what you ask for.

What I didn't know at the time is the
rest of this teaching that says:

You always get what you ask for.

I know this because I got what I most wanted in my
life at that time: an enlightened spiritual master.

The second teaching I received was:

Nothing is as it appears.

Some people are not who they appear to be, and some
places are not what they appear to be. Occasionally we
are surprised, but rarely shocked, by this. For many
years I was not what I appeared to be, even to myself.

So let me share with you my story: that of
finding the enlightened master within.

I LOVED WHAT I COULD LOVE

I had a natural passion for fine clothes, excellent food, and
lively conversation about all matters that concern
the heart still alive. And even a passion
about my own
looks.

Vanities: they do not exist.

Have you ever walked across a stream, stepping on
rocks so not to spoil a pair of shoes?

All we can touch, swallow, or say
aids in our crossing to God
and helps unveil the
soul.

Life smoothes us, rounds, perfects, as does the river the stone,
and there is no place our Beloved is not flowing,
though the current's force you
may not always
like.

Our passions help to lift us.

I loved what I could love until I held Him,
for then — all things — every world—
disappeared.

—St. Theresa of Avila
(translation by Daniel Ladinsky)

INTRODUCTION

The story I have to tell you is a true mystery. It maps my search for a spiritual guru and my path toward enlightenment. In my search, I discovered where both of these experiences could be found.

With all my heart I asked for a spiritual master, even before my mind knew what I wanted. I was an educated, well-taken-care-of woman who had it all — marriage, children, and a very comfortable life. But I didn't have what I truly longed for: enlightenment. I believed enlightenment was a state of unending bliss and the end of all personal suffering. All of my seeking led me to believe that a spiritual master was the one who could take someone to enlightenment. While my desire for something more came at an early age, my search eventually became more mindful and focused on finding a sage who would give me clarity, divinity, and freedom from the illusions of this existence.

I found one. And once I found one, I spent six years as his disciple. I lived a life unknown to everyone in my world at the time, including my husband, my small children, my family, and my friends. The entire experience took place in an "ashram without walls." We didn't have to go to India. We were modern disciples, awakening in the modern world and using every modern experience to become awake. For many years, I felt like I had won the "spiritual lottery."

I found myself smack in the middle of an ancient-style "mystery school," an immersion school for spiritual transformation that involves handing down ancient knowledge revealing the mysteries of ascension, alchemy, creation, and enlightenment from previous spiritual masters. It was beyond anything I had ever heard or read about. I remember searching the Internet for information about mystery schools and never finding anything remotely close to what was happening in this particular world. A beloved modern master, Osho, writes at the end of his *Book of Secrets* about the final stages of enlightenment in which one must have a master to enter the true mystery of God, beyond the mind. Even this could not begin to describe this bizarre human experiment in Austin, Texas—one hundred and twenty willing disciples who lived a life completely unknown to everyone on the "outside." To this day, everyone involved disbelieves, to a certain extent, that what happened in our group even occurred. For some disciples this lasted almost eighteen years! Three days ago, I was stopped in the street by an ex-disciple who wanted to let me know that he was "not doing well" and didn't know if he would ever be OK.

How could something be perceived as brilliantly transforming to some and completely diabolical to others? How can someone who "has it all" be seduced into trading it all in to serve a master? What makes someone susceptible to blindly following? What is the psychological foundation for secretly following and protecting a self-proclaimed guru?

My childhood made me the perfect candidate. I had a life-long addiction to seeking love. There was emotional neglect in my household that resulted in my deep need for attention and for feeling special. I wanted to be saved from suffering and I wanted to save others from it too. Part of me struggled with this double-sided savior complex.

When I heard about a book called *After Ecstasy, the Laundry*, I connected with it immediately. After many transformative experiences, I would come home to deal with all the mundane aspects of life including making school lunches and going to the dry cleaner. It didn't always feel like a major contrast because one of the teachings was that life was a seamless meditation, no matter what the activity. The outer will always change but the inner stays connected to love always. This connection to God becomes your freedom from suffering, no matter what your external situation might be at any moment.

What is still an enormous mystery is how this group managed to stay a secret from the world for almost eighteen years. Actually, there were several times that this "cult" was exposed. But each time it was too far-fetched for people to believe. With every exposure, it was dismissed as preposterous.

I felt guilty about keeping my participation a secret. However, "making a higher choice" took precedence. Always. My children were too young to understand what I was doing at the time. My husband and I separated before I became involved. Regardless, I was always told to "choose the highest and everything will always work out."

I also had to protect the identity of The Master because, I was convinced, history had shown us that masters are always persecuted. This was a Mystery School and, therefore, unexplainable. What follows is my experience of something truly unbelievable as well.

This book is an invitation to join me on my path toward enlightenment. I hope that my journey will illuminate your own. I long for the one experience that will change things forever—the single moment that will leave me devastatingly fulfilled. I was looking for a "once and for all" experience. There are those who say we are already enlightened and that we just have to choose it in the moment or realize it. Okay, I'm not talking about that kind of enlightenment. I'm talking about the kind where a moment happens that shifts everything.

I've heard it described as, "I woke up one morning and there was no self" or "In a moment I found myself to be the bird whistling outside, the tree it was sitting on, the earth the tree was attached to, the totality of existence." I am talking about the kind of experience in which you truly are the love you've been looking for, completely—where you feel the awe of God and merge with Source. You go to a place beyond duality where everything is an illusion, and where a singular, intellectual point of view can be set aside. I suppose I could go into the age-old pondering of "What is enlightenment?" I could research all the definitions from countless schools of thought and arrive at many different answers. I just read a good explanation on my tea bag tag. It says:

When you know that all is
light you are enlightened.

I'm not an academic by nature, and I'm not interested in all the definitions of enlightenment. It is the experience I am looking for. I look forward to the day I will read this and say, "That was how I saw things before I was enlightened!"

So while I am waiting, I just live life. Fully.

Sometimes I can taste it. It's as if enlightenment is just barely under the skin. I feel it living just around the corner, only a breath away. One author described it as "You go around the whole world searching for your car keys, and then after years, you look down only to realize that the keys have been in your hand the whole time." How can something so simple be so difficult to attain?

Now, this is the real mystery.

Almost every decision I have made in my life has had something to do with bringing me closer to the greatest love there is. And while searching, I have not always seen the love right in front of me. I have made many decisions in what I thought at the time was "choosing the highest," but right now I am not so sure. There are those I have hurt, such as my children and family, by not always being available. I lied and justified my actions by seeing myself as taking the high road. There are those to whom I did not speak my truth in order to protect the identity of the master.

Many lives were shattered beyond repair by The Master. There are times when I did not speak out about this and justified it because it was not happening to me personally and was not my experience.

To all of these people, I humbly apologize, from the bottom of my heart. To anyone I hurt in any way, I am truly sorry. And to those I am unaware of hurting, either through indifference or any lack of compassion, I apologize as well. I never meant to harm anyone. There were choices I made in the moment for what I believed to be necessary for enlightenment. I believed this enlightenment would be my part in saving the world. Let this book be an extended apology and an invitation to explore all that I have kept hidden for so long.

With all that said, I still would not trade the experience for anything. The truth is that in spite of all the controversy and scandal, I grew. I expanded tremendously and can see how the total immersion in this group taught me about myself in ways that may not have happened otherwise.

In the end, I am grateful.

CHAPTER 0

Here Wow

This is a memoir.

I wrote this true to my feelings, my beliefs, my longings, and my experience at the time. I wrote this before I had ever heard any of the following words: *The Spiritual Hierarchy, Channeling, Galactic Origins, Star Beings, the Inner Sun, Ashtar, Metatron, Sacred Geometry, the Merkaba Body, Planetary Ascension, the Galactic Federation of Light, 11.11.11, 12.12.12, DNA activation, sound healing, energy vortexes, the vortexing of the crown, twin flames, star children, rainbow children* and *crystal children.* Now, these words are part of my daily vocabulary. It's what I eat for breakfast.

Little did I know that the speed of evolving consciousness would be so extraordinary. This perspective of what can happen in only three years since my six years in the Buddha Field gives me tremendous excitement about the times we are living in. Things are only accelerating.

We are here, Wow.

I wrote this when the path to liberation was through meditation and through a guru. My timeline at this point (which also follows my books) is:

The Buddha field: Volume I: The Outer Teacher

The Modern Muse: Volume II: The Inner Guru

An Ascension Diary: Volume III: The Multi-Dimensional Self

However, even with this vibrational frequency upgrade that is making all of these things such as planetary ascension possible, there is still something that remains the same: the steadfast, solid, and unending love emanating from the human heart. My heart still loves, breaks, longs, melts, leaps, thuds, skips a beat, bleeds, purrs, expands, contracts, and opens no matter what happens.

CHAPTER 1

Kissing a Stranger

"Close your eyes," he said in his soft hypnotic voice. "Step forward until you feel someone's breath on your face. As you feel that breath, place your lips on that unknown person's lips.

"Kiss."

"Kiss deeply."

"When you're finished, slowly pull away and only then can you open your eyes to see who it is you are kissing."

I opened my eyes. It was Creed. Whew! How did I get so lucky? I had always wanted to kiss him. And the kiss was good. So was his smell and the feel of his breath on my upper lip. It was a fortunate kiss, but others were not so fortunate.

Randomly paired were women with women and straight men together, all at various ages. I cringed as I watched an elderly man kiss a twenty-year-old girl, unbeknownst to each of them. It was funny, entertaining, suspenseful, and riveting. Imagine all the people you know in a random kiss mix, such as your uncle with your best friend or your grandmother with your female roommate. You get the idea. Welcome to the Buddha Field.

This was a typical class for the Buddha Field, the secret mystery school that had become the center of my life. It was around Christmas time, and I remember I had taken some mistletoe to the garden that morning. Upon seeing the master, I waved the mistletoe.

"We should all get a kiss!" I coyly suggested. However, I did not know that later that night there would be an exercise in kissing someone without having a clue as to who it might be out of 120 people in attendance. The exercise was about not having a preference. And being so firmly planted in meditation that nothing can shake you. And about not having an idea about something but being totally innocent in the moment with it. And about finding the divine lover in everyone.

Besides, "through total surrender comes total freedom," our master explained. That one phrase can rule the world. And it did rule my world, for a while. As well the world of my fellow disciples who were willing to do anything to be free, to find enlightenment, and to transcend the world of suffering.

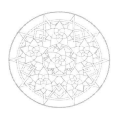

CHAPTER 2

Eleven and William

Two things happened when I was eleven. I met William, my future husband, at a baseball diamond. As our eyes met, I was struck by our meeting. Even as a girl, I knew he was involved in my destiny. Second, while at the library, I saw a book called *Man's Search for Meaning* by Viktor Frankl. I had never seen a book like this before. I opened it to the page with a pyramid of words created by Maslow and at the very top of the pyramid it said "Self-Actualization." Then it went on to say that there was a state beyond this called "Transcendence." Without a doubt in my mind, I decided and knew at that moment that this is exactly what I wanted in life. But even stronger than this thought was the feeling that came over my body. It was as if all the cells in my body rose, separated, and suspended themselves in a chorus of knowingness, like a symphonic crescendo on a nano level, an otherworldly body harmonic.

Growing up, my religious experiences were zero. I always wanted to understand why others were so crazy about religion, but I just didn't get it. When I accompanied my family to a Methodist church, however, I was overwhelmed with deep sadness often to the point of tears. I would cry for no reason during a service, always wondering, "Why am I crying?"

Early on, I started drawing and would spend hours alone, falling into a peaceful and rich silence, always disappointed when it was time to speak again, as if I had to betray my silent lover to do so. I also started ballet when I was eight, feeling ecstatic joy at getting lost in movement and classical music.

These moments of body knowingness came at random times, and I can remember them all. I would just find myself in them. They would occur at very ordinary moments, such as when I was sitting in a car and eating a bagel. When I was younger, I had no frame of reference for ecstatic energy, so I would think, "Wow, now is a good time to die because I am completely happy, and there is nothing more to do here."

My parents were from a long line of hard-working, self-sacrificing people who didn't really expect happiness from life. That was the way it was back then—a generational flaw. I'm certain we were not the only family who suppressed our feelings as a way of life. I think all children, at some point, blame their parents for the difficulties of childhood. But now, as an adult,

I know that I chose exactly the right parents for my spiritual evolution. And I thank them for that. I may have suppressed my feelings. But, later, I struggled to find them again.

My two sisters, my sweet mother, and I suffered from emotional neglect. It was innocent abuse. My father simply did not know better. Yet, no matter how oblivious he was to it, he had a huge impact on the decisions and choices I would make over the next decades of my life.

I made above-average grades, so I could get away with virtually anything. Mostly I snuck out to wild parties, usually at some wealthy kid's house whose parents were out of town. We were middle class in lifestyle and mind-set, so I took any opportunity to be away from my uneventful surroundings.

In school, I was an overachiever. I belonged to the art club, loved writing, and excelled in all subjects. Even college was easy for me. I graduated magna cum laude, and I didn't even know it until I looked at my diploma when it arrived in the mail. I wasn't interested in going to graduation. At that time anything institutional, like sororities or clubs, didn't mean a lot to me. The idea of those sorts of clubs horrified me because of their rules of conformity.

While I was still in high school, I had wild boyfriends, and we experimented with drugs. I had a boyfriend who was a bigtime marijuana dealer who, years later, was mysteriously found dead on his boat in the Caribbean. Before he died he was sort of king of the "surf mafia" in Corpus Christi, Texas. As a teenager, there was nothing to do but surf, lay on the beach, hang out, and experiment with sex and drugs. While I personally never dove deeply into the drugs, I liked the forbidden-fruit quality of it and all the cute boys that were a part of the scene. We were tan, we all had long hair, and I lived in my bikini. My boyfriend made me a custom surfboard with a big cluster of airbrushed purple grapes.

Although I managed to create as much mischief as possible, it was only in reaction to this overwhelming sense of middle-class mediocrity. I felt trapped. When I wasn't with my forbidden friends, big fun for me was going to Cloth World, where I could find a huge bolt of gold lamé fabric. For me, gold meant "glamorous," a far cry from the life I lived with my parents. I begged my mother to make me an outfit out of it, and she did. She did that for me a lot—always sewed a new outfit for me and helped me express myself in ways that were available to me. I remember many times lying on my mother's bed for hours in my underwear while she sewed and I waited for fittings. She had a glass paperweight that had belonged to her grandmother with a yellow rose encased in it and a black velvet bottom. I must have stared at that piece for hundreds of hours on the bed, lying on my belly, kicking my legs up in the air and waiting for my mother to take my measurements or fit me. She would let me pick the patterns and fabric and did that for all three of her girls. If one of us had a date, she would sew buttons on our outfits up to the last minute before we walked out the door. She was so proud of the way we looked and always insisted we look our best. She would say "Now, *that* is smart-looking." Like so many mothers of her generation, she gave her life to us, and we were grateful. Probably not enough, but we thanked her then.

While my mother was at home with us, my father was out on oil rigs in the Gulf of Mexico. He was the quintessential absent father. He was gone all the time so it was just "us girls." My mother devoted her entire life to us.

When my father was home he could be downright mean, and it scared us. While he never hit any of us, he withheld affection, attention, kindness, and tenderness. Neglect was his weapon, and it hurt. I wouldn't understand until years later why he was the way he was.

Christmas was one of the most painful times for us, because while my mother nearly killed herself and sacrificed to make certain we got everything on our Christmas list, my father almost never had a gift for her under the tree. My mother was generous in so many ways; I just couldn't understand why my father didn't reciprocate her emotional generosity.

CHAPTER 3

An Act of Kindness

"Here it is if you need it, Janis," my father said to me as he placed a coffee can filled with sand next to my bed. He put it there so I could spit into it if I needed to. I was lying in bed at the age of seven with pneumonia.

At that moment I was speechless, as he had never tended to me in a nurturing or caring way, much less be in my room. This was such an unusual gesture of compassion, I actually felt guilty that he did something for me. Affection and any expression of love were extremely rare.

One day later that summer, after I arrived home from camp, he asked me if I had found my gift. I panicked, first thinking I had done something wrong. Then I felt confused because he didn't give gifts. Then a horror came over me. I remembered finding some Beechnut chewing gum in my lunch box earlier in the day, and not knowing what it was, I gave it away. I realized I had given away my father's act of kindness, and I was racked with guilt. I couldn't possibly tell him I had given it away, so I lied and said that I had found it, thank you very much. I tell this story because this is one of the few acts of kindness I can remember from my father growing up. Such was the state of affection and emotional neglect in my childhood.

My joy came from quietly being in my room, drawing and creating. I spent at least a year on one drawing called "The Prisoner," done in a very detailed pointillism style.

My greatest fear was being a hostage of mediocrity or settling for anything that wasn't the A experience.

My greatest humiliation was being ignored by my father. My childhood wound would always be about trying to "get" the love, which always seemed to be out of my reach. Of course I was an A student to get my father's approval, even if it was just a nod of recognition. This imprinting would prove to play a major role in my search for love, my search for self-love and my search for divine love, which are all basically the same thing. Psychologically, I was programmed by my father to believe that love was withheld, affection was withheld, and that I was unworthy of love.

Seeking love was the natural state of my childhood. Love came in very small doses of attention from a man who had all the power, and those tiny doses were hard to get. You had to do everything right and still, that was no guarantee. This ultimately would set up a condition of viewing the patriarchal figure as controlling, withholding, and emotionally abusive. One was meant to follow someone who had absolute power. This created a situation in which there was always an enemy in the house. My two sisters, my mother, and I bonded in survival but were forced to compete for attention as well.

My early life conditioning set up my acceptance of a never-ending quest. One looks for things forever. One seeks but doesn't find. This becomes the whole foundation and motivation for living. If I don't have to try and get love, then what will I do? If I stop seeking, then what will I be? If I am not on a quest, then what am I doing with my life?

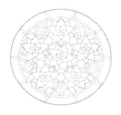

CHAPTER 4

David

The first time I met David, I was sixteen and a junior in high school. We met at a mutual friend's house. He was seventeen, a senior, and sort of an offbeat character. He drove a Triumph motorcycle and lived on an actual yacht in the marina with his father, who was a famous trial attorney. He had gorgeous, long, blond, curly hair that looked like a giant crown of angelic ringlets. He was naturally athletic and had a silly, yet manly demeanor. Although he was young, he had a strong sense of who he was—quirky, extremely intelligent, and highly creative. He was his own person.

There had been a rumor around town that David had once tried to jump off the Harbor Bridge over a failed relationship. After we got together, I noticed that his mood could quickly spiral downward at any form of rejection from friends, family, or me. He also sometimes drank too much. But at sixteen, I hardly knew the warning signs of an emotional condition that could quickly and tragically get out of hand.

My parents did not approve of David or anyone unless they were clean-cut and short-haired, but that did not stop us. It was the Montagues and the Capulets all over again.

"You cut all your hair off!" I screamed in horror as I opened the front door of my house the night of my older sister's wedding. I was very nervous about asking him to come with me to the wedding because I knew my parents strongly disapproved of him. We were hard-working, serious middle-class people. He was rich, didn't have a job, looked like a hippie, and lived a life of leisure and play. They had no idea he was so kind and thoughtful and made me feel safe and loved.

A huge grin took over David's face, and without a word I knew he had cut off his hair to win my father's approval. He was serious about me. I was genuinely surprised when my parents actually allowed him to come over, since I had been practically forbidden to see him. I was touched and a little afraid at this extreme behavior. I felt responsible for him giving up his beautiful hair.

Later that night at the wedding reception, David was still not feeling welcome by my parents, especially my father. I never knew what transpired between the two of them, but David desperately wanted me to leave with him and go down to the "boat," as he called it.

"I can't leave the reception, my parents will kill me! And you know they won't let me come down to the boat," I pleaded. But there was no changing his mind. He left without me, and I suddenly had a horrible queasy feeling in my stomach. I called our friend Steve and told him what had happened, asking if he could go and check on David. My gut was telling me to go to him.

"He'll be fine, Janis, don't worry," he offered.

The next morning I woke to the vision of both my parents towering over my bed, waiting for me to wake up. In an instant, I knew everything.

Every cell in my body shot through the roof with panic, shock, and adrenalin as I began to scream.

"NO NO NO NO NO NO NO NOOO NO NO NOOOOO NO NO NO" was the chant I could not stop screaming as I rolled up into a fetal position for weeks, stopping only to take tranquilizers and occasionally eat.

He had committed suicide. We had been dating not quite a year, and he was my first serious boyfriend. I loved him, and I completely blamed myself.

Maybe if I had gone with him that night. Maybe if I had seen the signs. Maybe I could have urged him to get help. My self-persecution was intense and endless. The sense of guilt was crippling, and no clergy, no friends, and no family could prevent me from feeling personally responsible for a young life cut short. What I didn't expect was what happened next.

Losing the love of my life was horrible. Being blamed for it was almost too much for me to bear. Not only had I lost my best friend, but suddenly I had become the target of widespread gossip around town. People struggled to understand how this smart, handsome, promising young man could do such a thing. Without answers, they blamed me.

The funeral was a scene straight out of *The Scarlet Letter*. My parents gave me Valium, and I don't remember much from that day other than the hundreds of eyes on me. Two days later, and in the midst of the greatest pain I had ever known, I fell asleep in an armchair and had a dream.

In the dream David walked right into the room where I was sitting in that armchair and sat down next to me. I spoke to him. "Thank God. I have been dying to talk to you. I am so happy to see you!" This was my first embodied visitation. Like many experiences from this point on, I was not completely aware of the spiritual implications of what was happening to me.

"It took a lot of effort for me to be able to appear to you like this so you would know it was really me," he said. "I want you to know that I really didn't mean to commit suicide. I was playing around. I was pissed off. And I was drunk. It was an accident. I didn't mean to do it, and I am so sorry. I hope you forgive me."

I suddenly felt very loved and managed to relax in that dream moment.

"I just want you to know that I love you," he said to me.

He got up and started to walk away. I panicked and screamed, "Don't go!" My heart and soul cried out to him not to leave. The thought of never seeing him again was unbearable.

He turned around and grinned. With a goofy laugh he said, smiling, "You know I can't stay." Then he was gone.

I woke up and felt disoriented *knowing* I had actually talked to David. Though I was sadder than ever, I was grateful he had come to me. Over the next year, I spent a lot of time trying to heal and being with David's family, especially his father. I clung to him.

CHAPTER 5

The Dream

Our definition of power changes with maturity. At one time, power for me meant wealth, prestige, and the so-called power to create my own world. At the time I believed this, I was at a "what's next?" pause in my life that seemed to surface every few years. This pause had a soundtrack, and it was Peggy Lee's song "Is That All There Is?" I know that's a very old song and was even vintage when I first heard it. But it came up occasionally in life, generally when I had achieved some sort of outer success, like graduating from college. (When you have inner success, the song is more like "You Mean There's All This?")

I had career and financial success from my own graphic design firm. I had started it one year after I graduated from the University of Texas as a fine arts major. After graduation I was hired as an art director for an advertising agency but found it hard to follow the authority of a boss, even though I loved producing the work.

I was young, and I wanted to know what I was supposed to want NEXT. I remember thinking that I wanted someone more powerful than me, as arrogant as that sounds. Or as my girlfriend put it, "You need a kinky CEO." So I placed my order with the cosmic waiter.

And of course it was delivered. He was a handsome, young, successful, and powerful CEO. Of medium height and build, with dark hair and greenish brown eyes, he had the distinguishing looks of Richard Gere and the boyish charm of Kurt Russell.

Plus, we had actually met when we were eleven years old and had had a brief stint as boyfriend and girlfriend. That first LOOK we had of each other at the baseball field then is frozen in my mind for eternity. I have a theory that you can always remember the very first LOOK of those you truly love. It is the moment you are arrested by something that stops you in your tracks. It remains a permanent image etched onto your mind.

Years later, he showed up in my office looking for a graphic designer. He hired me and we began a series of business meetings.

Before I knew it, I was flying around in a helicopter with him surveying his projects in South Texas, and very impressed. Our business meetings became long dinners until finally the ice was broken and the courtship was on. On one of our first dates, he sent a white limo all the way to San Antonio to pick me up and then had me driven to Corpus Christi for dinner. William always did everything in a big way. He was my knight.

He was also my strength during the devastating death of my older sister.

I was living in San Antonio working as a designer. I loved my life. I had my own graphic design firm, and financially I was doing really well. I was constantly traveling, I was single, and I had a groovy apartment. Though I was a workaholic, I worked with the best of the best in finance, insurance, oil and gas, and restaurants, and regularly ran with the big boys making deals happen and working at the top of my game. It was an exciting time, and I felt like I was mastering this part of my human experience in order to understand the mechanics of the physical world, what motivates people, how people make money, and what's important to them. There was a happy chaos about this time when suddenly my fast-paced world stopped cold.

One night I was watching television when the phone rang. My father called. He didn't call me that often, so I was concerned. He wanted to talk to me about my older sister, Celeste. Before I could say anything he said, "Something's happened to Celeste. She's in an ambulance and they can't get her to breathe. They're taking her to the hospital and it's not looking good."

For a brief moment, what he was trying to explain to me did not register. I was in shock.

"Penelope is with her. Let me call you back." My younger sister, Penelope, lived in the same town as Celeste, Corpus Christi.

Staring blankly at the TV, I sat there waiting for the next phone call. A few minutes passed and the phone rang again.

"She didn't make it."

It was my Dad. More shock—a shock that lasted for months.

My sister Celeste was only thirty-six. She died of a ruptured spleen. My family always knew that my sister's physically abusive boyfriend was responsible, but we couldn't prove it. We knew she had recently neatly folded his clothes and put them on their bed. When details emerged, we believed he had kicked her in the stomach while wearing his heavy motorcycle boots. The image of that man attacking my sister after such a simple act of serving has never left me. He didn't go to jail, but later admitted to us that he had killed my sister. He went to jail on separate aggravated assault charges, and I suppose there was a bit of justice in that.

We were horrified that he showed up at the funeral and acted the grieving boyfriend. But in the midst of this heartbreaking scene, a flurry of monarch butterflies hovered over the enormous wreath, full of spring blooms and roses, we had chosen for her. I took one of the roses home and, miraculously, it stayed fresh and dewy, like the day it was cut, for over a month. People came to my home and marveled at the longevity of this huge red rose that I believe was imbued with my sister's loving essence.

As children, Celeste was an incredible athlete and dancer. She was goofy, bubbly, and unselfconscious. She was a cheerleader, a homecoming queen, and a talented performer. In many ways, she was my mother's favorite. After she died, I discovered a letter in my desk that she had sent to me a year before. At the time she had mailed it, I hadn't wanted to read it. Her life had spun out of control. But that day, I opened it and read her personal confession of every horrible thing she had had to do to survive. There were drugs, abusive relationships, recounts of what she had had to do for money to support her habit, and so much more. I couldn't finish it—and never did.

Two months later I felt compelled to drive from San Antonio to Austin for a therapeutic massage a friend had recommended. At that point, I needed to do something to put my mind at ease and care for a body that had cried so many tears. The minute I got on the table, I began to sob deeply. The masseuse stopped and said, "I don't really know anything about your trauma, but there is someone here who wants to speak to you through me."

I had no idea what he was talking about and had not yet been introduced to the concept of channeling. But deep in my heart, I knew that Celeste was about to communicate through him. The room suddenly filled with this intensely divine loving energy. It was like we were in another dimension, much higher than the physical one I had signed up for that day.

The masseuse began to speak my sister's words. She thanked me for all the times I had tried to help her and wanted me to know how much she loved me. She explained that she wanted me to help heal my family.

It was beautiful and profound. When it was done, the therapist told me that he had never experienced anything like that before in his life. He was a large man, and he said the energy nearly physically knocked him over. I took to heart every word she shared with me that day, and I was finally out of shock.

As a result of Celeste's death, my sister Penelope and I suddenly became much closer. It was a time in my life when my spiritual journey had taken an unexpected turn into mortality, grief, the afterlife, and karma. I read *The Tibetan Book of the Dead,* which further expanded my perspective on the nature of physical death. Maybe Celeste's death was a part of the cosmic order. Maybe she knew she was going to die. Maybe there was a destiny that I had yet to understand. But what I did know for certain was that Celeste's soul was alive, free, and present in my life. To this day, she is a comfort to me and a guide. She is not dead.

After we buried her, there was the issue of going to gather her belongings—at her murderer's house—that had not yet been taken into custody. My family turned to me to take care of this, as usual. I usually played the role of the family "hero." At that moment I realized how much I had played the savior and how much I wanted to quit playing this role. So I said no, and stopped. Or so I thought.

After this tragedy and during the grieving process, I found comfort in William, who kindly looked after my well-being and that of my family's. We spent many weekends quail hunting on the King Ranch, alone in vast spaces of land, getting to know each other. It was here that we became engaged.

My mother loved him, and my father liked him, which said a lot. I loved him too. We married in Houston and had a formal dinner reception at the Ritz Carlton Hotel. Unlike most weddings that have a frenzy of women getting ready together, I spent a peaceful day alone, savoring my life and feeling grateful for William. I felt like a princess marrying her prince on an impossibly romantic and enchanted evening.

Eventually, we had a stately home on Rice Boulevard in Houston, Texas. The house faced Rice University, and the entire boulevard was lined with old majestic oaks whose top branches grew together and formed a complete canopy of shade over the street. Our backyard looked like something out of *The Great Gatsby*, with a long pool surrounded by lush grounds, and just enough staff. Yes, I now had a staff, which sounds like quite an adjustment to make. But it was amazingly easy, thanks to William. Soon after we moved in, I became pregnant. It was not something we were trying to do, but here it was, part of the flow. It was what was NEXT.

"You look first. I can't bear the suspense," I said to William one night as we were lying in bed. I was holding the sealed envelope that contained the sonogram and the sex of our child.

"OK, I'll look first," he said as he opened the envelope. Tears came to his eyes as he softly said, "It's a boy."

I looked at him, and we both cried tears of joy as the pregnancy became real in that moment. We were so happy.

We spent weekends at friends' ranches. We traveled effortlessly between country life and big cities. I tried on dresses at Barney's in New York that cost thousands of dollars. William was happy to buy them for me. I selected a Chanel dress that was so pretty I still have never worn it. Around that time, I attended a ball at the Chapultepec Castle in Mexico City. This was our life.

I remember how the birth of our son completely opened up our hearts even more to love. In fact, that is probably why we hurriedly got pregnant with our second child. This was a time of marital bliss. I thought it would always be like this. But after two years, my marriage began to show signs of stress.

While it would be easy to divulge every detail of its collapse, it is not a new story. People grow apart, they want new things, they simply cannot give any more. They try everything to keep it all together so the children will not have a broken home. But what I realized is that our home would already be broken if its stewards were broken people.

The slow collapse of my emotional life within my marriage left me feeling defeated, depressed, stuck, and eventually numb. I considered leaving, but was too afraid to survive on my own in this situation. I thought I could settle for survival and my comfortable life. Like my father. And my mother. But William had his own dreams, too. And enough was enough.

After our daughter was born, she brought so much joy that we just sort of settled into an arrangement of still living together as man and wife and still sleeping together, even though things were never really the same between us.

Having small children was challenging for me. I often thought something was wrong with me because the job of tending to small children was frustrating and not very fulfilling. It wasn't a question of loving them, as I loved them absolutely and unconditionally. It was the nature of the work: the constant diaper changing, feeding, cleaning, and cooking. I harbored self-hatred about myself as a mother, until one day a wise friend told me something.

According to Native American lore, there are two types of mothers. One is the Earth Mother. She thrives in the role of caretaking, nurturing, and tending to babies and children. The other is the Rainbow Mother, who lives to inspire her children. Both are equally important, necessary, and valued. Knowing this set me free. I was ready to accept myself and my style of mothering. I loved telling my children stories, doing artwork, reading and playing with them. I was fortunate enough to be able to hire someone to help me with a lot of the hands-on caretaking.

I remember how much William worked. More work meant more money, prestige, and the whole package. But the work did encourage the distance that kept growing between us. I started to gravitate more toward the inner world and people who were like-minded.My artistic nature was reemerging.

It was a Sunday, and I was lying on the olive green silk velvet sofa in our exquisite home in Austin, Texas, where we had moved. It was a six thousand square foot, *Architectural Digest*–worthy house in an upscale neighborhood known as "Pill Hill" because of all the doctors in the area. There was a ribbon of a driveway that wound its way through some tall woods, ending up at a very modern concrete barn. The walls were giant slabs of concrete, exposed inside and out. You entered through an understated front entry into a grand space. There was a very modern kitchen with a big counter used as an altar space for flowers and mandalas, which I changed every few days. The living room was cathedral scale in size and sound quality. One wall was solid glass, overlooking downtown. It was filled with an eclectic mix of furniture—eighteenth-century sconces and candlesticks, a giant gold baroque marble table that was once the entry table of the historic Driskill Hotel downtown, old paintings, faded silvery champagne-colored antique Oushak rugs, cowhide-covered throne chairs, and period Empire side tables. It was bohemian royalty meets ultramodern. The master bedroom was filled with Prussian blue silk damasks and pigeon-blood-red velvets along with emerald green original Fortuny fabrics. There were silver stripped old mirrors behind the bed with bedside lamps made out of eighteenth-century reliquaries, complete with bone fragments from saints. The large window behind the writing desk looked out over acres of woods, and the trees created a green lace curtain. This is still my favorite bedroom ever.

It was my birthday, and I wasn't getting any attention from my husband. As if I needed anything. I was feeling very sorry for myself. How could I possibly want *more?* I had what people thought was the perfect husband, two beautiful children, the dream house, money, and I didn't have to work unless I wanted to. It was just too inconceivable and shameful to imagine that I still wasn't happy. But I wasn't.

In fact, I was lying on the sofa experiencing a back spasm between my shoulder blades where my "wings" attach. I couldn't move. Having just moved to a new city, I called the only person I knew to help me find a body worker. I was referred to Marcus, who could see me in two hours.

As I walked up to the office building, I saw a beautiful beaming smile mounted on an Italian looking face. Marcus, a handsome young athletic man, held the door open for me. As I passed through this portal, we had the LOOK. But it was not a romantic look of love. It was actually something I had never felt before.

We went inside. He helped me with my body and all the stress it was holding. I cried as he worked on me, and he wiped away every single tear. We didn't say a word. It was OK for me to feel whatever I was feeling.

Later, we talked and I asked about him. I was surprised to learn that he volunteered to take care of a paraplegic. What a concept. The idea of such selfless service was foreign to me within the context of my life, where money could seemingly solve everything. In this new reality, service and devotion was the new currency.

He was actually the first person I met who was a devoted meditator. This was not counting Jeff, who I knew in college and who was on a very austere spiritual journey, reading Gurdjieff and eating only brown rice. Marcus' life was very simple. It was about less and not more. He had a certain energy about him that said he wasn't looking for anything from the outside. He was like a light bulb, and I was the moth.

I found myself looking for excuses to go and see him. I would bring him food and talk to him about meditation. I shared what I was looking for, but felt self-conscious because I didn't have the language to express my deep spiritual longing. I didn't know what he had, but I wanted some, more than anything else. Was it peace? I asked him if he would teach me how to meditate. He said no, but he did refer me to someone who would help me to become strong enough to avoid future injuries.

One night, I had a profound dream.

I was frantically running through the many rooms of my house, trying to find the source of a loud alarm going off. Where, oh where, was that alarm coming from? Who had set it? Why was it so insanely loud like a siren? Where did I get such a clock? When did I get such a clock? I think I may go crazy if I don't find it. I have been through every room at least twice, and I am at my wit's end. Finally, I walk into my bathroom. Sitting on the corner of the vanity is an antique Buddha turned into an alarm clock, just sitting there ringing and shaking. Aha! I found it! I reach around the back of it and turn off the noise. Then I wake up from my *dream and realize it is time to wake up from* the *dream, and I roll with laughter at the cosmic comedy of the dream.*

Yes, it was time to wake up from the dream. I had definitely been living in one.

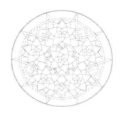

CHAPTER 6

The Training

I took two really big drags from my cigarette before I chunked it on the asphalt. I didn't even bother with a breath mint as I strolled into the training room. It was a small and cozy private gym downstairs from Bella, a colorful and trendy hair salon on Fifth Street. As I saw him, I knew the name certainly fit. He looked like a cross between a great Indian warrior and a Greek gladiator. In fact, I later learned he was a runner-up for the role of Wind in my Hair in the movie *Dances with Wolves*. He had spent time in Hollywood only to trade in the actor's life for a life devoted to meditation. He was tall and had long, black, straight hair, a large chest, a thin waist, powerful legs, and a strong chiseled face. I was a little nervous and suddenly felt overweight and out of shape.

Thus began my training with Maximus. There was no chit-chat. Each session was highly focused. If you are focused on every breath, there is not much time for conversation. My physical transformation began that day. I first noticed it at my daughter's sixth birthday party. I saw a reflection of myself in the glass window at a pottery studio, not knowing it was me. I saw a leaner, younger-looking version of myself and was momentarily surprised that it was my own reflection. I have always been petite, but had become a very round, puffy petite with no muscular definition when I started training. I had always worn my brunette hair about shoulder-length, but I started letting it grow long, beyond my shoulders. The style was long, straight, and shiny, instead of "done." I was wearing less make-up and more tank tops and was feeling like I had a new body. I was drinking water constantly, my skin looked better, and my eyes looked greener.

For the first time I gave myself permission to be as disciplined as I wanted to be without any judgment or guilt about excellence. I realize this is the opposite of how most people feel, but I was afraid of shining too brightly. I started to live in my body in a new way. It was becoming finely tuned. I really loved knowing what to eat, when to eat it, how to have a really thorough program that was a lifestyle and not just a diet to temporarily lose weight. It was difficult in the beginning, because basically four different meals had to be prepared at dinner. The kids liked different things, I was eating just protein and veggies, and my husband required a square meal. Because I wanted to please everyone, I indulged my family's differing tastes.

Maximus' first teaching was that 70 percent of how you look and feel is diet. That was staggering to me at the time. He never gave me any goal too impossible to achieve at any one time. He seemed to have a knack for challenging his clients but not overwhelming them. The first thing he had me do was to write down everything I ate for a week. That exercise alone gave me a clear look at what I was actually eating versus what I thought I was eating. I was pretty much in denial of all the little chips, sodas, bites of cookies, bags of movie popcorn, and other snacking I was doing. After looking it over, he suggested that I stop eating complex carbs at dinner. I could have small amounts at breakfast and lunch, but no later than that. He also suggested I improve the source of complex carbs, eating more sweet potatoes and brown rice in small amounts instead of bread, grain products, corn products (uh oh, no popcorn), or anything with white flour. And the most important dietary change: no sugar. He was ferocious about no sugar and believed that it is only an evil that sabotages your mind, metabolism, and mood. This is still a challenge to me.

His second teaching was about consistency. What you do every single day counts. I remember watching him eat the same thing day after day for years, even making fun of him, until I realized that consistency is very important. Thirdly, he was all about protein. He believed in protein at every meal: chicken, fish, protein powder, or eggs. And no alcohol. He was lenient on portions, always telling everyone to "Eat when you are hungry, and never starve yourself!"

I didn't feel I could ever give up smoking and weekend drinking. Whenever I brought them up, Maximus would say, "Don't worry, it will go away." I would have never believed him in a million years because I was such a twenty-year, pack-a-day nicotine addict, but he was right. It actually did go away. A window popped up in my head one day that said, OK, now is a good time to jump through and escape this habit. A little golden opportunity was granted. Whew, it was close.

I never really brought up my personal life, but after about a year, it started leaking out. I was very attracted to the same qualities in Maximus that were similar to those in Marcus. He too was a meditator. He also helped a paraplegic. His life was simple and about having less, not more. He was consistent, and he didn't party. In fact, I had no idea what he did with his personal time. He seemed committed to his practice that involved every aspect of his life. And there was never much drama. He showed up always in a peaceful, focused state.

Once I actually admitted that there were problems in my golden cage of a marriage, his response was always, "And what is your part in all of this?" It was always up to me to take responsibility for everything in my life.

I did take responsibility for my unhappiness. There was mounting stress in the marriage and mounting frustration within me. I took a bold step and announced to the family one day around Christmas that I was leaving for a week to go on a silent retreat, at a monastery in South Texas. All I wanted was silence. I wanted everything to stop so I could actually hear myself again.

Alone with my thoughts for a week, I went crazy. I was so powerless over my uncontrollable mind that I came to decision: I would commit to meditating every single day, forever. And I would find peace. At this point, I didn't even know that an ecstatic life was possible.

One day William was out of town, and I was going to a movie. I asked Maximus if he wanted to go and he said, "Sure." The movie was *American Beauty*, a classic tale of suburban angst. It felt like a mirror being held up to my life to show what "settling" had really cost me. Afterward we sat in my car for hours and talked. The dam had broken, and I was forced to look at my feelings. I had numbed myself, sold out, settled, shut down, and abandoned my true self. I wondered if I could even still hear my soul. I had given all my power away to a man, and the role I needed to play in order to keep him. Where was my authentic self hidden?

From then on, I spoke openly to Maximus about my life. He became a confidant, but he never took my side. He was comforting because he gave me his undivided attention. He was totally present. But he was both my champion and my challenger. He wanted me to see my part in everything and take responsibility for my life.

Lying in the bath at night, children sleeping and the house quiet, I would sometimes call Maximus and complain, ask for advice or just express myself. I was finally being heard and not feeling ignored! Many times the subject would come up of my desire to find a teacher or a guru. Where could I find someone with whom to train not just my body but my entire being? Where was the wise loving sage I was looking for? I really had it in my head that I was ready for *The Teacher* or *The Mystic*. Since I was ready, why hadn't he appeared?

Maximus' advice about my marriage was always "Don't do anything."

"Even if I truly think I don't want to be married anymore?" I asked.

"That's right." Something was happening that I could not get my head around. A transformation.

I was drawn to something that Maximus had and I wanted it too. I began to meditate. I really had no idea what that meant, but I would just sit quietly with my eyes closed, burning sweet Indian nag champa incense as my mind wandered endlessly. It actually took months before I realized that my mind was a constant stream of video, like watching a movie. Occasionally there would be moments of peace, but they were few and far between. After watching this day in and day out, I suddenly had the realization that *I* wasn't my mind. I had heard that before, but it was never my experience—until one day it *was* my experience. The mind was just going to do its thing regardless, but beyond that constant chatter was a place that was eternal. It wasn't the video but the one watching the video.

Even with this awareness, which can be a big spiritual turning point for anyone, the mind was impossible to control. I decided to get some help so I looked up "meditation centers" in the phone book. I called around and ended up at the Shambhala Meditation Center, where they gave free meditation instruction on Saturdays. There, I learned a simple technique of counting my breaths. I would count each breath up to four and then start over. With each breath I became more and more aware of the quality of my breathing. It is amazing how difficult this simple exercise is. I rarely got to four without my mind wandering. My meditation technique would change over the years, and it is still changing now. But for this period, this technique was alarmingly simple and more difficult. I would do this at least thirty minutes every morning and every evening, with a different experience at each sitting. Sometimes the mind was completely active the entire time. At other times I experienced a deep peace for short periods.

But still I wanted more. How could I dive into what Maximus and Marcus had, even more?

I dove into yoga. I went to New York and met David Life and Sharon Gannon, who had started Jivamukti Yoga. After my first class with Sharon, I was totally in love. What I didn't know was that she was sharing Truth in her classes. It was the mother's milk for which I had been thirsty my whole life.

I had found a wonderful definition of Truth on a tea bag just that morning. It read, "Let your heart speak to another's heart." Truth is a powerful force that transmits a holy vibration, and my body knowingness went off like a car alarm when I heard it. So now, this was it.

My framework of thinking at the time was grand scale and entrepreneurial. My idea was to take this Jivamukti Yoga and franchise it all over the country. Who would not want this? It was like the elixir of life. The nectar of the gods. At the time, I didn't know that Truth could actually be found other places.

Back in Texas, I e-mailed David immediately. "I am supposed to help you franchise Jivamukti Yoga to America, or at least Texas for now." He actually replied right away: yes, he was interested.

That was enough for me. I was back on a plane to New York to put this deal together. The meeting was first with Sharon, his partner, and it went well. I was to go back to Texas, meet with my franchise lawyer, and get back to them with a proposal, which is exactly what I did.

The more we got into working out the details, the harder the project became. The reality is that it was like trying to capture lightning in a bottle. Truth is not a commodity to franchise. It is alive, it exists in the Now, and it has to be delivered fresh and steaming, hot out of the oven from someone who is connected to the Truth. Before this point, I thought that Truth described experiences that were framed by honesty and rightness; it was a description. The Truth I came to know is actually a holy vibration that transmits real energy. The project came to a standstill because neither party could figure out how to bottle Truth and market it to the world. It can't be done.

Meanwhile, back at home, tensions were mounting in my marriage, and I found myself very disconnected from William. There was disharmony in the house, and I didn't like the way it was affecting the children. Children thrive in a happy environment, and I was always very focused on providing this for them. Mariela, our beloved housekeeper, was always a fountain of love. But I was the mother and the woman of the household. It was my job to maintain harmony in the home.

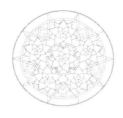

CHAPTER 7

The Divorce

It seemed like too much space had grown between William and I for us to find each other anymore. Our family meals barely happened, and he seemed even more immersed in his work. We didn't know how to enjoy each other. I couldn't bear to drag him to marriage counseling another time, because all the other times had failed miserably. We took a trip to South Beach, Miami, to rekindle the flames. This actually worked for a little while. But I felt increasingly sad and powerless, like I was on a sinking ship with no control.

The idea of divorce was horrifying to me, so I just numbed myself and told myself how lucky I was to have so much freedom and such a generous husband. I would become racked with guilt every time I considered divorce, especially because of the children. I just kept shutting down more and more, performing my duties and telling myself that it was okay and that I was fortunate to be taken care of.

But one night, I happened to be outside around seven thirty in the evening, and I saw a sunset. I realized that I had missed seven years of sunsets, always putting kids to bed or preparing the evening meal.

I desperately wanted William to listen to me about meditation and the turn my life had taken. But the truth was that we were no longer interested in the same things. After a while, I just quit talking about it, but found myself mentally comparing his interests with those of the new people in my life such as Marcus and Maximus. I liked that they accepted me and listened to my woes.

I agonized over what to do. One of the hardest parts was the actual decision to get a divorce. It would affect so many people, mostly my children, and I couldn't think only about myself. I felt like my parents might never forgive me for this. And I truly loved William. We were just on totally different paths. I second-guessed myself for a long time and agonized over the decision until one day on the radio I heard Sting's song "Let Your Soul Be the Pilot." In an instant, I had my firm answer and resolved to proceed with the divorce. All the cells in my body rose and harmonized in a knowing chorus of "Yes." That was it.

We both knew it was over, but still there were many late nights sitting at the kitchen table crying, explaining, expressing, and trying to figure out a way to make this happen. I was firm in my resolve to get a divorce. It was tough for both of us, but eventually we came to an agreement. It makes me very sad to this day.

The children were five and seven at the time and so completely innocent. I had tried to stick it out for so long because of them. The thought of hurting my beautiful children and scarring them for life made me feel extremely guilty. I will never forget the look on their little faces when I told them. Even though they didn't quite understand divorce, they understood something devastating was happening.

The actual legal proceedings went well, thanks to William. He said I could get a lawyer if I wanted. I said no to the idea of getting one and told William that I trusted him to decide what would be fair. Neither one of us really wanted a lawyer, and many of our friends and family considered this course to be absolutely stupid, especially for me. I told William that I knew he would do the right thing, and he did. He did more than that; he was fair and generous, a man of his word. By honoring him with my absolute trust, he honored me.

The divorce itself, however, was tough. On the actual day, November 17, I remember feeling like I had been hit by a truck. Nothing really prepared me for the tidal wave of emotions. I wrote: *Today I was divorced. How do I feel? Grief-stricken, calm, in awe, tearful, honorable, safe and secure, tired. Amazed at what we have done. Proud of both of us. But mostly I feel compassion and love for William.*

CHAPTER 8

Private Eyes

After months of a very dark period and feeling like I was living in a cave, I started spending more and more time with Maximus. One day while training, he was eating a bran muffin. Unbeknownst to him was a big crumb on the corner of his mouth. Out of the clear blue, I had the impulse to lick the crumb off his face. Without thinking one single thought, I leaned into him, and slowly ran my tongue over the corner of his mouth to get the crumb. I couldn't believe what I had just done. A flood of energy swept through my body like a wildfire. Where had this desire been all this time, and why did it appear in such a flash? Then we had the LOOK. Uh-oh. I think Maximus would also describe it as a defining moment. So, from then on, the energy between us changed forever. We became more than friends.

I parked my car at Central Market and couldn't wait to make the call. I was dialing Maximus's number as fast as I could to invite him over for dinner. I had the house to myself for a few days, and it was the perfect opportunity.

"That won't work," was his reply when I excitedly rolled out the invitation.

"Why?" I wanted to know even though I was risking sounding too desperate. "Because I'm busy," was his simple answer.

"OK," I murmured, not wanting to stoop and ask what he was busy with. I followed with, "Well, what about Saturday night?"

"I can't do that either," was all he said.

This was getting really awkward. Then he finally said that he would not be spending any time with me over the weekend, period. He felt like he didn't owe me an explanation, and that I should not be asking for one. I felt a lump in my stomach. Wow, who was this person who was suddenly so inaccessible and secretive? Where did my loving friend go? Well, this was Maximus, who had the same standards in life as in training, which was never to settle or veer off the course. I just didn't know what course he was on. I felt devastated and like I had entered the Twilight Zone. This was really strange behavior.

I swallowed my pride and asked him what night he could come over.

"Tuesday, I could come," he answered.

He took off his shoes at the door, walked in, and paid absolutely no attention to his surroundings. I thought for sure he would comment on the house. It felt weird, like two very different worlds colliding. The old world of luxurious surroundings, and the new world of simple living. As it was once said to me by a wise friend, "It's not how much you have, it's how much you enjoy what you have."

Maximus presented himself as someone not very materialistic. He was never impressed by "things." Once, I gave him a Gucci backpack for his birthday and he barely wanted to keep it, but I insisted.

Once inside the kitchen, I did not feel the urge to ask him if he wanted to see the house. We went to the living room to meditate. We got comfortable, sitting side by side in the dark with our eyes closed, meditating. Or rather, he was meditating, and I was trying to meditate. His focus was on enlightenment (I assume), and my focus was on him. The room was lit by the sparkling city lights of downtown Austin in the distance. It was difficult for me to sit for hours on end, but I tried. My mind was filled with thoughts about Maximus's powerful still body, sitting next to me. I felt heat rising and desire soaring. I realized he would probably never make the first move, and I was going crazy. I thought about leaning over and kissing him but didn't want to be aggressive. If he wanted to kiss me, he would, I thought. But I was going crazy.

After at least two hours of "mind-a-tating" about wanting him to touch me, I leaned over and brought my lips as close as I could to his, without touching. I know he could feel my breath and I could feel his breath. I drank in his smell and started to feel intoxicated with even more desire. This was entering some kind of super sensitive, sensuous zone where all atoms change. This lasted maybe a minute until there was nothing else possible to do except slowly put my lips on his.

At that moment, both of our bodies opened to each other, and all the desire that had been cultivated over many months came flooding out. This first kiss was insanely delicious, and we just melted into each other. Without saying a word, he took me by the hand and we went into my bedroom. Before we lay across the bed, I took a moment to light some candles in the silence. We made love that night for hours, unlike anything I had ever experienced. The thought came to me that I was now completely ruined by his lovemaking and would never be able to settle for anything less than this again.

Later that evening, I saw an image of our naked bodies in the darkened mirrors. His large bronzed back was mounted over me, slowly making love in the candlelight. I couldn't believe that I was actually in this beautiful scene of these two bodies merging. Losing myself deeper and deeper into him, it just kept getting better and better. This was just too good. It was so far beyond my wildest imagination, my only thought was, "I'm fucked."

We never really spent that much time together because of his all-consuming schedule. He was busy every single night except for Tuesday and Friday. At first, I was the cool aloof girlfriend who wasn't too interested in the details of his schedule. But after a while, and as we became more intimate, my mind took me for a ride. What could he possibly be doing five nights a week, sometimes until two or three in the morning, that was "none of my business?" He would actually use those words whenever I asked questions he didn't want to answer. It was starting to drive me crazy. I didn't want to appear insecure, but I could not come to a peaceful justification. I had to take matters into my own hands.

I couldn't believe that I was actually considering this option. But not only was I considering it, I was proceeding. It seems like quite a big step to hire a private investigator, but there were no mutual friends I could ask, nor did I want to risk losing him by needing to know everything about him and his life. It wasn't so much that I suspected other women; I wanted to know what I was missing out on. What was his secret life? Was he a male stripper? Was he in a cult? I suspected it was a spiritual group, but I didn't want to expose it, I wanted to join it.

"Hello, is this Norman the private detective?" I said as I looked around to make sure no one could hear me. After he replied yes, I began to tell him the story without making it sound like a suspicious girlfriend. But there was no masking the reality of the situation.

"So what's this guy into? Drugs, gay sex, cult stuff, Nazi shit, devil worship, prostitutes?" It was clear that he had seen it all, and nothing would surprise him.

"Oh, God, no. Nothing like that," I said as my mind was trying on all these new possible scenarios. "I'll give you his whereabouts, and you can just follow him and see where he is spending the majority of his time," I replied. And so I did, even though it felt really creepy, like I had somehow crossed a line. But who would ever find out? I hung up, knowing that information would be arriving soon. I was free to focus on my next move into the yoga world.

CHAPTER 9

India

N ow that the yoga franchise was off the table, I wondered what I should do with this beautiful new
friendship with Sharon and David, whom I adored and
admired. They were in Austin for a yoga conference, and I
was really enjoying the time I had with these two yoga rock
stars.

We were having lunch one day when Sharon asked, "Why
don't you come to India with us? You can train with Patthabi
Jois, one of our gurus. Our good friend Sting will probably join
us too. It will be great!" David agreed with her. "Yeah, that
would be great."

Wow. I had to think about this one. This felt like THE invitation I had been waiting for. Was I finally going to meet my teacher? And how perfect was the timing?

I also saw this invitation as a way to establish some independence from Maximus. I felt like a beggar much of the time in our relationship. I was always waiting for more from him. I was very dependent on him because he played the role of my teacher, showing me a new way of taking care of my body, my mind, and my spirit. It was scary for me to feel so drawn to someone. So while he was often like a nurturing mother, he could also be a tough father. Always there for me with consistency and love on a daily basis, he could also be rigid and hard, with no flexibility. I was used to having a stern father figure in my life, as that was what I had grown up with. I became frustrated because he never deviated from his schedule or his eating patterns. I wanted to be spontaneous. Well, that didn't work with him. A movie on an occasional Friday night was about it.

He was the first person who started talking to me about the "ego." The ego is the part of the mind that always wants more and wants to be in control—the smaller self, so to speak. It is usually what drives us until we begin to recognize it and let the larger self drive.

I was always wondering, "Where do you get this stuff? Who is teaching you this, and where does this knowledge come from?" And his answer was usually, "Who wants to know?" While this would totally piss me off in the moment, it did make me think about where my curiosity was coming from. Was it a genuine desire to know, the need to be in control, the child wanting validation, or any number of ego-driven desires? I was ready to crack this mystery.

CHAPTER 10

The Neon Affair

She was tall, blond and supermodel beautiful, wearing a neon-colored bikini top with yoga pants. She was, without a doubt, making eyes with Maximus in the hot yoga class we were attending. At first I thought, *You have to be kidding. No way is that woman so blatantly looking at Maximus, smiling and holding his gaze for such long periods of time.* My mind went crazy as this went on the entire class. He would smile back but not as blatantly as she.

After class, I couldn't wait to ask, *"Who was that?"* And so I did. Even though we had just learned about the tendency of our mind to get "sequestered" by a thought, I still could not turn off the voice in my head that was totally distracted.

"Who's the one who wants to know?" was his reply.

"I do!" was my obvious answer; I was annoyed by the spiritual presumption of his question.

"She is a woman I know, and it has nothing to do with you, so that part of your mind that is the comparing female mind is the one who wants to know, or it's the little girl who is afraid Daddy is going to love someone else. It's for you to ask yourself."

I was too mad and hurt to admit it, but I did feel like the little girl who was going to lose Daddy to someone else. It was also the comparing mind who saw her as prettier than myself. It was all aspects of my ego, my smaller self.

Such was my relationship with Maximus.

Later, I did find out that these two had a brief affair. He and I had already started seeing each other when she popped up on his radar screen and they got together. For whatever reason, things did not work out with her, and it ended as quickly as it started.

When I found out, I was deeply hurt and confronted him. He was sympathetic to my feelings and said that he understood if I wanted to leave. But I didn't want to leave, and for some reason it was easy to forgive him. I knew he was not in love with her. The fact that I could just let this affair go showed me that I was making a decision based on the love and the energy that was present, and not based on pride or judgment. It was certainly a step toward freedom and evolution for me. At least, that's what I thought at the time.

CHAPTER 11

Out of the Mouths of Babes

Our personal relationship began to flourish. I felt so lucky to be spending time with someone who I felt was there for me emotionally, holding my hand the entire time, so to speak, and guiding me into new spiritual frontiers. His biggest gift was consistency. He was always available to talk and encouraged me to meditate, follow my eating plan, and stay the course. He would listen and talk about every emotional issue that arose for me, no matter how small.

He was very cautious about not imposing himself on my children as a new daddy figure, but was very natural with them, like a kind friend. The four of us didn't spend a lot of time together. But on the occasions he was around the house, he played the guitar and sang to them. I could tell he absolutely adored them but just wanted to let things evolve naturally, as they did.

It was important for me to integrate my children with my spiritual life. Up to now, my life as a mother and my life as a spiritual seeker had been separate. It was time to bridge the gap and include them in my journey. Soon thereafter, I received evidence that it was time.

"Mommy, I have a question I want to ask you," my six-year-old daughter said to me one night while I was tucking her in after story time.

"Who am I? I mean, who am I, really?" she asked as she looked up at me with her cherubic face. Taken aback by this serious question, I scooped her up in my arms and hugged her.

"That is such a wonderful question! It makes me so happy that you would ask that," I gushed. I wanted to answer this difficult question in the best way to serve her in her innocence. It was such an opportune moment for me to share truth.

"That is a very hard question, my dear, and one that I spend my life working on. But here is my answer to you. You are God, and you are going to spend most of your life realizing it. I have devoted my life to that question and finding true happiness." That was my answer.

From that moment on, we saw each other in a way that transcended our family roles of mother and daughter; we shared a special bond and secret the way fellow travelers or seekers sometimes do.

With my son, all you had to do was look in his eyes and see the depth of his being. He was born an old soul, wise beyond his years. Even as a toddler, he had a magnanimous spirit, freely giving his Cheerios in the park to anyone and everyone. The maids in the park had a nickname for him in Spanish, *Papo,* which meant the Pope.

As I would watch them sleeping at night, radiating purity, I felt so blessed to have these two little ones along for my journey in this lifetime. It always felt like they were kindred spirits who chose me to be their mother for a reason. I did not want to disappoint them. And I wanted to be a good mother to them— someone they could be proud of.

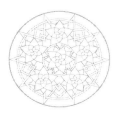

CHAPTER 12

The Buddha Field

One evening while sitting on my living room floor, I decided to tell Maximus about the plans I had been cooking up to go to India with David and Sharon. I laid out the fruits of my good fortune, having been invited to go, and asked his opinion.

Dead silence.

"Can you believe this stroke of fate? I'm going to India, and I am so scared and excited. Finally, I may meet my teacher," I repeated. Maybe he hadn't quite heard me.

Still, no response.

Finally, I said, "What are you thinking?"

Long pause. "You don't need to go to India to find your guru. What you are looking for is right here," he softly replied. Well, thousands of questions arose in my mind. *WHAT? He's right here? Where? Who?* It's funny how with all these questions came a lot of the answers that had been right in front of me the whole time.

This is where life started to become surreal. This is where you may think you are beginning to read fiction. But I promise, you are not. This is where you come to a fork in the road. One way is the known, and the other way is the great mystery. I was into the "no rules apply" area now. So began a tornado of questions that seemed only to create more questions.

By this time in my life, there were a lot of new characters. A psychic once said to me, new people will be coming into your life in droves. One day I looked up, and the droves had already arrived. It was like an empty restaurant that had completely filled up with people while you were caught up in a conversation and not looking.

Aurora, a healer, was one of the first of a long string of colorful people to enter my life. She had been recommended to me by Marcus. I had once asked Maximus about her, and he said he thought she was a good healer, although he sounded a bit tentative. She dressed like a goddess, and was a nutritionist and homeopath with her own TV show. She worked with energy, oils, nutrition, massage, colonics, supplements, flower remedies, a whole toolbox of new toys to me. One day, while in her bedroom after a homeopathic treatment, I saw a photo of some friends of hers and asked her about them.

"Oh, those are some of my friends in the Buddha Field," she replied nonchalantly. Upon hearing this simple sentence, an explosion of energy shot through my body.

"What? What is a Buddha Field?" I asked, as I was already visualizing a field planted with Buddha heads perfectly in rows like a divine crop being grown by some even more divine being. Why didn't I know about such a thing? And how perfect did this sound as something I definitely wanted to know more about? I had recently attended some Buddhist meditations in Austin and was very attracted to the teachings. I had also read several books on Buddhism, as well as many other books on eastern spirituality.

The look on her face was even more surprised than the look on my face. "You mean Maximus has never mentioned this to you?"

"No," I replied with shock, hurt, fear, and confusion. As she spoke, I realized she had said something she was not supposed to say. As she backpedaled, she did offer, "Oh it is just this group I meditate with, that's all."

Well, that was really all I needed to hear, and I let her know I would love to be in a meditation group. As I expressed this, all I got back was a dismissive, "Oh the group is not really meeting right now." Something was really amiss here.

Too late. The cat was out of the bag. I now had at least a small piece of the puzzle with which I could work. I had a combination of curiosity and feeling left out. I definitely wanted to know more. Besides, this is what I had been looking for. And I was sure there must be a teacher somewhere in the mix.

Approaching Maximus with my newfound knowledge didn't get very far. All of his answers were vague, either because there was something he didn't want me to know or because he was protecting me from something. He encouraged me to focus on my meditation and trusting that whatever I needed would be provided at exactly the right time. Well, this took a lot of trust.

"Who is the one who needs to know?" was his annoying response yet again. It was so hard to not be angry and to truly ask myself that question. The real answer was the ambitious one who wants to be in control and know what is going to happen. At this point in my life, I desired a guru or a master teacher more than ever before, and the sense that I was around one only increased my desire. I felt I was so close to what I wanted most.

One day out of the blue, however, Maximus did say to me that I could write a letter to the unnamed teacher. Finally, I received the coveted confirmation that a teacher was among this group! I didn't know if he or she was dead or alive, living here or abroad. But I did feel tremendous relief. This was the milestone I had been walking toward for years now.

"Just express your true heart's desire in a letter, and I will make sure it gets sent to him," Maximus said. *So, HE must live somewhere else*, I thought. I jumped at the chance to make my own personal connection with the teacher. With great excitement that night, I went home, got out my engraved stationary, and wrote a poem.

TO: ?

The violins are singing their sweet song
Flowers have filled the room with their fragrance
My white dress is long and flowing
I am slowly walking down the aisle
Approaching my destiny
Ready for the veil to be lifted

That was my heart's desire, to be free of the illusion and merge with the divine. That was all I wrote on the page. I kissed the page, folded it, put it in an envelope, sealed it, and took my precious love letter to Maximus the next day.

On the rare occasions when we did go out, I was always very happy to be with Maximus. He had such a presence as well as being so attractive in a dark Mediterranean way. We attracted a lot of attention wherever we went, which my ego certainly enjoyed.

One Friday night, as we were walking into Gumbo's, a favorite downtown restaurant, Maximus quickly pulled me back into the street. "Uh, let's not go there tonight, there's somebody I don't really want to run into."

"Who would that be?" I asked.

"Oh, just somebody I meditate with who you don't need to meet," he replied, which just created more of the mystery. There was a feeling to all these theatrics that it would all be revealed in time, and that not knowing anything was for my good or my protection. It was as if something really great would be coming along, if I would just not be too curious.

So I wasn't too pushy but I was quietly more and more curious all the time. Things were really getting interesting.

There were a lot of other synchronistic things happening as well. In a very short time, I met more and more colorful characters. There was a yoga teacher named Jade. I found my way to one of his classes, which had spiritually mysterious undertones. I liked his reading of Rumi, the mystic poet, at the end of his class. I definitely had the feeling that many of the people there knew something I didn't know and that I didn't quite get. Maybe it was their knowledge of meditation. Who knew?

In Jade's class I met Sapho, a masseuse who was also highly recommended. I felt drawn to his lion like appearance and his playfulness. One day, I called to schedule a massage. This felt a bit daring, like there was something a little dangerous about receiving a massage from an attractive young man. But that didn't hold me back.

He lived in a modest house in south Austin with a roommate. It seemed so many people I was meeting lately had roommates. I figured that I must have been sheltered in my marriage and unaware that this was how many adults now lived. With roommates. Crazy.

As I entered his house, I saw his roommate. He was an extremely good-looking man named Creed. I wondered why Sapho did not introduce me, but he definitely did not want us to meet. Creed had a large Doberman pinscher who was roaming around the house.

I was hooked after my first massage with Sapho. It was a combination of great music, creative play, and deep movements. He would think nothing of standing on the table with his heel in your back or pulling you halfway off the table to get a good stretch between your shoulder blades. He was very spontaneous and in the moment. He was extremely gifted, with good healing energy and a personality I adored. While my body was not in any pain, I would receive this healing energy and was able to relax into a deeper sense of joy, appreciation, and love.

One day, he wore a rainbow-colored afro wig and stayed in the character of a total pimp clown, which made me laugh uncontrollably.

"This was my costume for a big Halloween party last night." I thought, *Now, that is a party I would like to be invited to!*

After the massage, an older blond woman with a definite territorial vibe showed up and planted herself in the room. She had the remains of cat-woman make-up on her face. Through her faded make-up, I could tell she was very striking.

I was surprised to learn that this was Sapho's girlfriend. She seemed a little cold and reserved. Another woman showed up, who was Creed's girlfriend. She was bewitchingly beautiful, and I could not take my eyes off her for a moment. She had long, thick, wavy honey brown hair that framed her beautiful large cat eyes floating above a full curvy mouth. She had the body and catlike movements of a ballet dancer and exuded goddess energy. *What an unusual and beautiful creature,* I thought.

I was struck by the attitude these two men had towards their "ladies." It was very reverential and respectful, something I saw as rare and quite attractive. These women were something to be cherished by their men. The men adored, listened to, and paid attention to them, something I had never really witnessed up close, certainly never in my childhood.

Okay, I'll take some of that too, I thought.

I was getting a lot of "recommendations" from my new friends. Maximus had suggested it would be really amazing for me to see a certain therapist named Jeff.

"You should try and get your name on the list, because he has at least a six-week waiting list," he offered. *Well, he must be good, so I certainly will get my name on that waiting list,* I thought. And true to Maximus's word, it did take at least that to get a meeting time with Jeff. Of course, I felt very lucky to have a chance to work with this therapist who was so in demand and had such a sterling reputation. An appointment was set.

I had just learned that Maximus and Jeff lived together, and it occurred to me that I had never actually been to Maximus's house. This would be the first time. I drove there baffled at the idea that I had never even considered visiting Maximus in his own home. He had such a shield of privacy concerning his life. And Jeff, the therapist, was his roommate? That was just too weird. Were there other roommates as well? When I asked Maximus about it, he said that he just liked to keep his private life, well, very private. Since I was part of his private life, it hurt that I wasn't treated as an insider in his world. But this was the theme of my life at this time. I felt like an outsider in so many ways. I had recently found had that he had once been a Chippendale-type dancer, which made perfect sense. He was sexy and good-looking. I could see that. I figured he just wanted to keep that information to himself. Or maybe he had stalkers.

He lived in a two-story brick house in a typical suburban setting. The only strange thing was the number of cars always parked out front, usually at least three or four. Inside, everything was very clean and well-kept. There was nothing strange except that four adults lived there, I later found out.

I disregarded those strange facts, as I was all set to begin the adventure of deep inner work. Nobody had actually prepared me for this therapy. It was not traditional, as far as my experiences went. First of all, it was not called therapy. It was "cleansing," a form of regressive hypnotherapy. I would talk about what was going on in my life, and then we would choose something to work on, like my relationship with my ex-husband. We would then take the upsetting feeling back in time to an earlier time when I had experienced that same feeling. Getting to the root of the feeling, I would then outwardly express the feeling, usually involving yelling and/or crying to release the charge or imprint. Afterward, I would feel great and "cleansed." I really liked this work, and I liked Jeff. He had a way of making you feel like he was your best friend and that you could trust him. There were a lot of people telling him their private business, so of course he must have been trustworthy.

At one point during our session, I asked him if he knew what I was getting involved in and if it was okay.

He looked me in the eye and very sincerely said, "Yes, it's like going home."

My phone rang.

"Hello."

"Hello, this is Norman." I immediately recognized the sleazy voice of the private detective I couldn't believe I had hired.

"I've got some news, can we meet?" Well, I didn't really want a face-to-face, but I would have to give him some money sooner or later.

"Okay. When and where?" I answered.

We met at the end of a cul-de-sac in some tract home neighborhood. You could use one word to describe everything about

Norman from his hair, to his clothes, to his voice, to his car: nondescript. I guess it was a good quality for his line of work.

"So here's what we've got so far," he started. "Sunday he went with a woman, arm-in-arm, to a theater performance at Global Theater. She was a brunette and medium build. Two hours later he left alone."

"On Thursday night he went to a residence waaaaay down south. The home is registered under the name Stan Collins, a sixty-year-old Austin resident. About seven that evening, a whole slew of cars showed up, parkin' everywhere, on the street and in the woods. Everybody went in carryin' some kind of black robe inside a grocery bag." I was so eager for this information, I didn't question how he would know the contents of a paper bag. I believed everything he told me.

"A lot of 'em were carryin' lawn chairs too. They all had this stuff hid in the trunks of their cars. They were in there for hours. About midnight, all the lights went off for about another hour or so. Then, they all came out at once like bats flyin' out of a cave, threw the stuff in their trunks, and left. Nobody said a word."

I would have to think about all of this. I didn't know what to make of this new information.

Meanwhile, I was falling into the adventure of becoming a yoga teacher. I had always been in love with dance and movement. I had taken ballet classes since childhood, as well as other forms of dance, so yoga felt completely natural to me, like redis-covering an old friend. And I had already fallen in love with yoga through the classes taught by Sharon and David, which were saturated in the vibration of truth. I was attracted to yoga because of the spiritual aspects as well as the physical ones, which is why most people are drawn to it. But since everything in my life was about finding a teacher, I wanted to experience the ancient art of yoga. I learned that according to the old yoga masters, the asana practice was created so that you could still your body in order to sit for long periods of meditation.

I began a teacher-training program with an older woman who lived near Lake Travis, in the hills west of Austin. I would go there every week and spend the day with her as we went over philosophy and discussed the books she had me read. The second part of the day would be spent practicing in her studio.

I spent some of my time with her crying over my divorce. For some reason, she had the nurturing energy that made me feel comfortable with expressing my feelings and letting them flow. And flow out they did. This was a tremendous healing time in that she allowed me the space to feel all the hurt, the grief, and the feeling of being lost after divorce. She also listened as I cried about marriage wounds and the wounds from my father, which were similar. At the end of the training, I felt like I had gone through an initiation of humility. I was humbled by her generosity of spirit and was reborn as someone wanting to offer myself as a selfless servant to those wanting yoga instruction. She was a gift. I trained with her for at least six months and got my registered yoga teacher license. After that, I signed up with Jade for more training.

His training consisted of morning meetings at his house with about five or six other local yoga teachers. It was an ongoing class for established teachers as well as for a few beginning teachers. We practiced teaching each other and giving feedback. I was nervous to instruct these well-known teachers, but I did learn a lot. There was also meditation at the beginning and the end of these sessions that had a strong affect on me. It was as if I could feel a transmission of peaceful energy.

After teacher training, I felt ready to begin a new life as a yoga teacher. I taught my first classes on the east side of town to a low-income neighborhood group for free. I got over stage fright there and really found the sharing of the present moment to be very satisfying. The hardest part was to empathize with people's pain and injuries, because that had not been my experience. Emotionally, of course, I could empathize, but physically I did not know what tightness or pain felt like in the body. I was very flexible and didn't have any pain in my body. It was easy to make the shapes of the poses, but the real journey was how you got there. It showed me how to quit "posing" in life – literally – and instead drop into the body and the breath. There was nowhere to go, no one with whom to compete, nothing to accomplish. There was just a diving into the present moment where everything happens, through the portal of the body and the breath.

Everything about it involved a new way of being for me. Teaching yoga was about being a nobody and serving all the love you have. I felt like I turned into the very best part of me when I taught yoga. There is also an element of surrendering to something bigger than yourself that always seems to take you out of your little self and into your bigger self.

At the beginning of every class, as I sat on my mat just being still and quiet, it would be like the beginning of a magic carpet ride. I never knew quite where it was going to go, but it was always an adventure. Something always took over and showed me the way in a new, creative journey. Sometimes class would be fun, sometimes so sacred you could feel divine energy filling the room like thick smoke. Teaching was and is a blessing.

Traveling to yoga conferences around the country was such a change from "vacations" where you just go somewhere and try to recreate your known life at home but add more luxury and different entertainment. I took classes, workshops, and trainings with some of the great lions and lionesses of yoga teachers such as Rod Stryker, Rodney Yee, Erich Schiffman, Angela Farmer, and Shiva Rea. Just writing their names brings up so much love, admiration, and gratitude for these beautiful and gifted yogis and yoginis who continue to inspire me on so many levels. Continued blessings pour from them to me and me to them. Always and forever.

Once, there was a yoga conference in Austin at the Hindu Temple. The food was horrible and could have been its own training called "How many ways can you concoct carbs and fat?" Honestly, I do not know how the devotees of the ashram did not all weigh three hundred pounds living on such a diet. While driving home from the conference and eating an apple I found in my car, I got a phone call from Jade.

"Hi Janis, how are you?" he asked.

"Great," I replied as I pulled my car over to stop driving. I wanted to be very present to this conversation.

"I'd like to invite you to something," he said.

Tingling energy started to flow through my veins. Was this what I had been waiting for? Was I finally going to solve this mystery? Was I going to be included? I really felt like the biggest thing to ever happen to me was going to begin now. Was I finally going to meet The Teacher, if there even was one?

"Can you meet me for dinner Tuesday?" It was not quite the invitation I was looking for.

"Sure," I said.

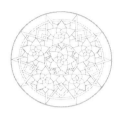

CHAPTER 13

The Invitation

At dinner, I realized that I was being interviewed ever so slightly. At one point, Jade asked me what I was looking for. As I poured my heart out about my sincere longing for a teacher, for something more, for something I didn't even have the words to ask for, I began to cry. I had no idea where these tears were coming from, but they soon turned into a river right there in the restaurant. I hardly ever cried, so this was a surprise. Without him saying the words, I knew I was being invited to meet The Teacher, and I was overwhelmed with gratitude.

I was told at this meeting that absolute discretion was needed. I could not talk to anyone about this. I knew this was the deal breaker. If I did not agree to complete discretion, I would not be allowed to meet The Teacher. Part of me dismissed the seriousness of this because I wanted so badly to meet The Teacher. But I could not walk away now. No way. I would just have to figure out a way to justify this to myself.

I couldn't even tell my own immediate family, ever. In fact, it was absolutely crucial to protect the anonymity of The Yoga Master (this was the first time I heard the teacher called by a proper name), as he did not want to be known and did not want to work with the masses. Some masters, like Jesus, are for the masses, and others are for a very select few who are ready to go the distance. This work would be too misunderstood, misinterpreted, and controversial.

After a very long silence from Jade, he gave me a sweet smile and said, "You're ready."

Driving home, I felt a pang of guilt about agreeing not to tell my own family about the existence of a yoga master in my life. Maybe I was crossing a line. I had heard about a pact with the devil, but was this a pact with the angels? The group feared an outsider would blow the whistle, call the authorities, expose the group, and cause The Yoga Master to leave town. There was a tiny voice inside me that knew this looked like a cult, even though I thought that word was scary and not applicable to us. Also, there had been rumors this group had moved from another state because of possible "exposure." We did not want to go through the same thing and look like idiots, and miss out on this experience of a lifetime or lifetimes. It seems crazy to think that something so wonderful should be kept secret. Although I did not know a lot about true mystery schools, this was a school, and it was certainly mysterious.

My daughter was five, and my son was seven at the time. Even if I told them, how much would they understand? I would explain my time away as all part of my yoga teaching and training. There were soon to be many teacher meetings, trainings, and classes to teach, the perfect excuse for the busy schedule of a devotee. But I could never have done it alone.

I was a privileged woman who had a staff when I was married to my husband. I had a gardener and a nanny who was also a housekeeper—Mariela. I believe Mariela was chosen by God to merge with my own family. Two weeks after my first child was born, she knocked on my door, mistaking it for another home's. I felt a deep kindred spirit in her immediately and hired her on the spot. She has been with my family for sixteen years. With Mariela, I finally felt a profound sense of harmony and household peace. In most cultures around the world, children have the benefit of villages, communities, and extended family to help care for and raise children. I was not raised with any outside help or extended family to support my mother. This was the first time in the lineage of women in my family where outside help and support was brought in to the home. It was a profound shift in understanding the isolation of being a woman today.

While not everyone can afford help, seeking a spiritual community helps connect women. There is a lot of synchronicity that happens when you decide to make your spirituality a priority. I could not have had this experience without the divine intervention of Mariela, and I am grateful for my circumstances that afforded it. As Paulo Coelho said, "When you want something, all the universe conspires in helping you to achieve it."

We all have our challenges in regards to love, health, money, and life purpose. This time around, mine just happened to be in the area of love, not finances.

Though I was highly in tune with how materially fortunate I was, my soul had stopped crawling and started running in the direction of seeking clarity, purpose, and awareness. My soul calling became even stronger when I became a mother. A switch had turned on, and I knew that I wanted to not only be there to do art projects and make cinnamon rolls, but to act as a spiritual role model to the two most important people in my life—my son and daughter. I felt I owed it to them and to myself to model a life of spiritual curiosity, creative exploration, and truth. These were the values of my family, and I was growing increasingly committed to understanding myself in order to find an inner peace and balance that my children could learn from and, I hoped, emulate someday.

In many ways, I consider Mariela a second mother to my children. She is about my age and size. We both have long, dark hair. Our relationship was always sisterly, even though we respected the traditional "attendant" role. Her style of serving was very humble and elegant: she could serve the president of any country and make him look good. Although she doesn't speak English, my Spanish was decent enough. The truth is we communicated on another level without words, beyond language. I see Mariela as an angel (even though she calls me her angel), possessing all the traits I lack, such as patience, consistency, and a willingness to be selfless. She never lived with us except when my daughter was born. And then, it was only for a few weeks.

People have asked me, "Didn't you feel guilty leaving your kids with the help?" They don't understand that she is more than that. She is my sister, my support, and my friend. And while other mothers might go to an office building, I knew my spiritual journey was a sacred job that would not only heal my life, but give my children the mother they most needed in theirs. I do not feel compelled to defend my parenting story, but in explaining it I hope other women can see that the work of the soul is indeed sacred for the life of a family.

"Can't I even tell my best friend?" I asked Maximus on the phone after my meeting with Jade.

"You know you can't, Janis. So why even ask?" he replied. He was so careful not to interfere with my arrival to the Buddha Field and had remained in the background lately, offering only support whenever it was needed.

I was invited to a Saturday night gathering. *Oh my God, what to wear? Who was I going to meet? Should I do my usual bohemian gypsy look or maybe a little more polished, as if going to church?* I wore my long hair down, groomed myself to a flawless shine, and wore a white silk billowy poet's blouse. Jade picked me up and drove me.

We arrived and walked in to the living room of someone's private home, filled with people. It was a beautiful tent-like Moroccan setting with candles and very attractive people sitting around mostly with their eyes closed in meditation. I was a sponge soaking in every detail, as my mind had been so curious about all of this for so many years. *Who were these people?* I knew only Jade. I was led to a seat. I instantly noticed a really beautiful young woman sitting on a cushion in the middle of the floor with her back perfectly straight. She was wearing an Asian dress with her hair tied neatly in a knot.

After a period of time, a woman came out of a bedroom and sat in a chair obviously arranged for a teacher. She was middle-aged, with short, dark hair and beautiful, expressive eyes. She looked like she could have been a schoolteacher or a former nun. There was water and a vase of roses on the side table. As she sat, everyone opened their eyes and listened. She silently looked around and let her eyes rest for a very long pause at each person.

Then she started to speak. I remember the essence of what she spoke about more than the actual words. I was moved and touched by the experiences she spoke of, about love and truth. I was thinking, *so this is The Teacher?* Well I never would have imagined this. After about an hour, guitars were brought out as well as songbooks.

"Okay, so this is your test," she said directly to me. I felt all the attention in the room turn toward my direction. I felt completely self-conscious, realizing I was the only new person in the room.

"You have to pick a song out. The song you pick will determine whether or not you can stay," she said.

The pressure was on as everyone glared at me in anticipation. I selected a tune from a giant homemade song book, and apparently an unpopular one. As I heard groans from everyone, my mind went into orbit with the "I have just discovered I have no clothes on in the classroom" feeling. I had failed.

After a short pause, everyone began roaring with laughter. The test was a joke. No one cared what song I picked. The teacher was just playing with me.

After the singing, a few people brought out *prasad*, which means "gracious gift." Someone would come and sit before you, offering a plate of something, usually sweet. But before you actually eat the sweet treat, you would have what is known as "open-eye meditation." This ritual would have different meanings for me through the years to come. Two people would gaze into each other's eyes for an indefinite period of time. At first, this was very confrontational, because there was an urge to say something, look away, smile, crack a joke, anything other than just be totally present, open and receptive to another person. I was told that when you look into the eyes of another, you keep taking your awareness back, toward the back of your head, so that you become less and less of this personality and more just a pure state of being. The person disappears, and the love shines through.

As I asked around, I got as many definitions as people I asked:

"To me it's like looking at a flower and being completely in love with the flower, but not wanting anything from it."

"For me it's about merging until there are no longer two people looking at each other, but one being."

"For me it's about bringing my awareness to the back of the skull where I become the witness and the personality dissolves, leaving only the One."

"For me it's like love looking at love."

Before we left, the beautiful woman wearing the Asian dress came up to me and delicately placed something in my hand. I looked down to see a wooden statue of Quan Yin, the Chinese goddess of compassion. How perfect.

On the way home, I told Jade I was glad to meet The Teacher, although I felt somewhat disappointed.

"What are you talking about?" he laughed. "She is not The Teacher!" He laughed even harder.

Confusion set in. "So when am I going to meet The Teacher?" was my next question.

"Through gratitude more is given," was his only reply. I would hear that line many more times.

More frustration set in. When I asked Maximus, he now acknowledged that there was a teacher.

"He is completely aware of you, Janis."

Wow. This sent a wave of excitement through my body. So it's a he and not a she. And he was aware of me? What did he know? What did he think? Did he have omniscient powers, to be aware of me? I had never really considered that the teacher might be a she, which surprises me now. My desire for a father figure was too ingrained to see at the time.

A few months earlier, I had read the great book: *Autobiography of a Yogi* by Paramahansa Yogananda. Yogananda's teacher was Sri Yukteswar. I instantly fell in love with him upon seeing his photo. He was a fierce fatherly figure of a teacher, steeped in mysticism, with a very direct style of teaching. And I felt like he had omniscient powers. He was only for those students with complete dedication, as he was very strict and demanded absolute commitment and discipline from his students. He had ran an ashram in India in the early part of the century and came from a great lineage of Masters. The first was Babaji, the "deathless" Himalayan saint, who is reported to still be in a body, four hundred years after his original incarnation. His student was Lahiri Mahasaya, who then became the master of Sri Yuktesar, who then became the master of Yogananda.

The relationship between student and master transcends all lifetimes and is considered to be a great blessing. Some say the teacher/student or master/disciple is the most important relationship of all lifetimes in that it is beyond a family of origin, beyond biology, and given for divine evolution. It takes a ready student to find his or her teacher and a soul's willingness to be woken up. The stories of these relationships are rich with teachings, both tender and severe. In *Autobiography of a Yogi,* I love the relationship between Yogananda and Sri Yukteswar as they met auspiciously and had a lifetime of complex experiences, which were ultimately transcendental as Sri Yukteswar appeared in the flesh to Yogananda after his passing. A great blessing indeed!

Gurus were more common in India than in America, and living with a master was a respected choice in the Indian culture in centuries past. This was new to me, as I had been programmed in America to believe that anything involving masters was slavery or "cult activity" and therefore evil. Early in my life, either because of the Branch Davidians or the Jonestown episodes, anything involving a leader of a spiritual group that was not mainstream religion was suspect and possibly dangerous to me. Terrorists were also associated with cults, especially after 9/11. There was the American media fascination with earlier spiritual teachers labeled "cult leaders," such as Osho and Muktananda, who were judged and persecuted by the media after scandalous eruptions. However, through the poems of Rumi and the teachings of Osho, I began to believe that mystery schools were of the highest order, and one of the fastest ways to ascend. I suddenly had no fear, and the truth quenched my deep thirst. Gurus were not "cult leaders" to me; they were spiritual necessities.

I never really struggled with the question of whether I was entering a cult because there was constant talk in the group of how privileged and evolved we were to have found a master to serve. How could that possibly be bad? We were searching for enlightenment, for God's sake! Also, there was the exclusive aspect to the group, meaning that very few were invited to join. I myself waited years. We never knew exactly what criteria The Yoga Master used to decide whether someone was invited, but it was usually done before he even met the person. *If it was a cult, then why wouldn't he let everyone join? What sort of people are attracted to such groups or "cults"? Wasn't it lost and confused people who were completely deluded or innocent and naive victims?* Well, I was none one of those, even though I was completely in denial of such a possibility. And even if this was a cult, were cults always bad? Many people believe that Christianity itself is the biggest cult ever known.

I loved the story of how Yogananda met his teacher, Sri Yukteswar. It was in an alley. An alley, a manger, a garage. Some great teachers like Sri Yukteswar, Jesus, and the mechanic in *The Way of the Peaceful Warrior* seem to come from humble backgrounds. Yogananda literally turned a corner one day and was drawn to this unknown figure in an alley, pulled by some kind of divine magnetism. This was the world in which I wanted to walk. I knew there were layers to existence beyond what was known previously or beyond what the mind could imagine. I knew there were other dimensions operating simultaneously with this so-called reality, but I had yet to find the keys.

Of course I was in love with Babaji, too. He is shown in photos and described as being eternally young, having a bronzed body, with long, dark brown hair and beautiful eyes. Maximus looked like him and even had a photo of him on the dashboard of his old Honda. Before I knew who Babaji was, I thought (and hoped) this long-haired man in the photo was Maximus's teacher. According to many, Babaji is still around physically somewhere in the Himalayas. Was it such a stretch to think of meeting him as well?

I will never forget reading about the initiation of Lahiri Mahasaya by Babaji, also in *Autobiography of a Yogi*. It is one of the most remarkable stories and worth reading. Lahiri was sent to a very remote post in the Himalayas for his job. Wandering around one day, he encountered Babaji, who was elated to see his disciple again from a previous lifetime. After being touched on the forehead by Babaji, Lahiri started to remember his last incarnation with his guru and even remembered the cave in which they were sitting. After acknowledging this reunion, Babaji then told him to rest for a while. Later that evening, he sent someone for him and brought him to a golden temple that suddenly appeared out of nowhere in the far reaches of the Himalayas. The temple was filled with mountains of gems and treasures. A feast fit for a king had been prepared. Every sense was stimulated beyond imagination. Many of Babaji's disciples were there in quiet meditation. Babaji told Lajiri that he wanted to give his old student his last desire, which was to visit a golden temple. So he prepared this heavenly celebration for him. After the pageantry, Lahiri was told to close his eyes. When he opened them, the temple had disappeared, and they were sitting in the very same sand in the cave in which they had been sitting the day before.

I knew it. Some masters had powers.

I felt I was getting closer to meeting The Yoga Master. Several years had passed since I had begun my meditation and spiritual practice. I had been regularly attending Saturday night gatherings known as *satsang*. During these meetings, someone would share or speak Truth.

These gatherings served as a sort of introduction or preparation for actually meeting The Yoga Master. We discussed basic guidance for developing qualities such as gratitude, one-pointedness (focus), service, and humility. The "three-legged stool" was the example of a good foundation for a spiritual practice and had three qualities: (1) meditation, (2) selfless service, and (3) keeping like-minded company, or holy company. There were guidelines about how to be around his body: very carefully, and do not touch! We learned how to listen if he spoke to you and how to make sure you were "in meditation" when you were around him, because he would certainly know if you weren't.

Many stories were told about knowing The Yoga Master, such as being with him, learning from him, and receiving love from him, even if it didn't always look like love. The stories told us how he worked in ways that could not always be understood. We learned what an enlightened being was, how the logical mind had to be dropped in order to enter this path, and how one must trust.

One very important concept was discretion. Basically, that meant NO ONE could be told The Yoga Master existed, including family members. Look what happened to Jesus when he became well known! What happens to anyone who is called an "Enlightened Being"? What does the government do when an individual has too much power? Devotees did not want The Yoga Master to suffer age-old persecution, and they went to extreme lengths to protect his anonymity. It was clear that he was not for the masses, but only for those select few who wanted to go all the way. Participation was by invitation only, and only he knew whose soul was asking for this or who was at a certain stage in his or her evolution and therefore ready to go further. There were many who weren't ready. These were the sort of people who might go public. They were not invited. His teaching methods were unorthodox and would be misunderstood by outsiders.

The world I was entering was meant to be an absolute secret. This didn't seem like it would be too hard, because all of my friends now seemed to be part of this company. But not telling my children was a different matter. I felt strange even though I was not "doing" anything other than attending Saturday night gatherings. I asked myself if they would understand what having an enlightened master in their Mom's life would mean. I didn't know, myself. Still, the fact that I was withholding anything from them caused me pangs of guilt.

The pages of the calendar were flying by like an effect in an old movie. I felt different. I loved being on a path and having "a practice." I loved being devoted to something bigger than me. I loved the reassurance that there was a reality beyond this that was ecstatic and joyful. I loved the fact that I could actually participate in and create complete liberation. And I loved feeling special and chosen: these were the intoxicating feelings that had been absent from my childhood and now drew me like a moth to a flame. Total freedom was accessible. This was enough to keep me going.

One day, Maximus invited me to a Sunday matinee performance at the Global Theater with him and James, his handsome, all-American-looking ex-gymnast friend. This was the place where Norm had spied on Maximus. I was intrigued. Of course I accepted and had the feeling that I should make a good impression.

Also present at lunch was another man, Nick. Nick was a tall, very good-looking, GQ-style hairdresser who was actually

Maximus's best friend. Wow. Something was changing, because I was now included in their inner circle.

I and the three Gs—the gladiator, the gymnast, and the GQ model—went to lunch and then to the theater. I felt like I was donning some very good accessories! I don't even remember the performance, but I do recall that I felt a lot of eyes on me when the four of us walked into the theater. It wasn't as though I felt important entering the room. But I knew people were checking me out. I wore all white and had taken care to be perfectly groomed from head to toe. I was slightly tan, with shiny, long hair and a sparkle in my eye.

The Global Theater is architecturally very interesting, designed like a modern Mediterranean Taj Mahal. It stands on a beautiful bluff overlooking the Texas Hill Country and its magnificent sunsets, which were part of the evening's entertainment. It is a well-known multicultural venue for performances including flamingo, ballet, tango, concerts of all genres, and opera singers. It is also known for its intimate performance space, accommodating only about three hundred people.

After entering, several strange things happened. First, it seemed like a lot of people knew each other in the audience. In fact, there were two young women that Maximus knew sitting right in front of us, but *no one* said hello to each other. I looked at Maximus and said, "Don't you know them?" He nodded yes but made no comment. When I asked him why he didn't say hello to them, he said, "Well, it's because I see them all the time." Just when I was about to ask him the next obvious question, the lights went down, as the performance was about to begin. It would have to wait.

At some random point during the intermission I had the urge to turn around. So I did. What I saw was to become an image etched in my mind forever.

I turned and saw THE BUDDHA FIELD. Talk about an aha moment! In the first second, I noticed the very back row of people and was reminded of *The Last Supper* by Leonardo da Vinci. The lighting was dim, and the people were sitting in a straight line with a pronounced energy radiating from them. I felt like I was seeing something reverent and holy. The people were stunningly beautiful and still. Most of them I had never seen before, but I just knew them to be the members of the Buddha Field.

My eye scanned the other five or six rows and I realized I saw a few people I recognized. THIS WAS IT. As things kept being revealed to me, I became more and more elated. At every turn, it was beyond my imagination. Instead of too good to be true, it was too good not to be true. I had really nothing to compare it to except my unfulfilling life at Methodist Sunday school. Growing up as a Methodist whose family only occasionally attended church was my only spiritual experience prior to becoming a seeker at age eight. Since then, I dove into reading, joining groups, studying everything from Buddhism to Sufism, attending yoga conferences, hearing speakers, and constantly seeking therapy or some sort of self-healing.

As Christmas was approaching, an older "disciple," as they were known, invited me for lunch. In fact, a few weeks earlier, when I first heard the word "disciples," a wave of energy shot through me. When I realized this was a possibility for me, the nobility and profundity of this pursuit was even more solidified.

We met at a macrobiotic restaurant one Tuesday afternoon. The atmosphere was very calming, and everyone was speaking softly. I had known Mara only briefly but felt very comfortable with her and admired her for her sincerity.

"I want to talk to you about something," she began soon after we were seated. So when I was least expecting it, and in a very nonchalant, matter-of-fact way, she asked me if I wanted to attend a Christmas celebration to meet The Master. After all this time, I finally received THE invitation to meet The Master. The moment was both unbelievable and straightforward. Wow, just like that.

"He is a fully awakened being," she said in a tone that felt like, *let's cut all the crap, and I will just give it to you straight.* I really appreciated that. I felt like she was someone I could confide in and trust. She said that she was "sort of" my sponsor and would be responsible for me. I felt a resounding "Yes!" and, of course, I accepted the invitation.

"Wear something really nice and bring a low chair," she said. "Be ready at 4:00 in the afternoon on Saturday." That was the next day. I rushed out and began scrambling to make arrangements for the children.

CHAPTER 14

Cinderella Goes to the Ball

Okay, here's a really big question. What do you wear to meet your Master? Dolce and Gabbana sounded good. Actually, it was the nicest dress I had, so I wouldn't have to obsess about what to wear. Or shop. Done. *I was ready.*

I was picked up and taken to an Old World–style grand ballroom near the University of Texas. What I am about to describe is a modern-day version of Babaji's Golden Temple story.

I walked in to what looked like an elegant and extravagant ball bathed in soft lighting, candles, the fragrance of thousands of flowers, silk tablecloths, ethereal music, and hushed, reverent speaking. The entire vibe of the room was overwhelming. There were long rows of tables set for a seated dinner of at least one hundred and thirty people. Guests were looking for their name cards and quietly settling into their chairs. Everyone was dressed in clothes fit for a ball, but with much more flair and drama. It was all very glamorous, almost like a fashion show. In retrospect, it now reminds me of Stanley Kubrick's film *Eyes Wide Shut*.

Although I didn't know their names at the time, there was Biba, who was a tall and striking brunette, dressed as a sexy Native American princess. There was Creed, who looked like Antonio Banderas, with his full, dark, long hair tied back, wearing a romantic lace shirt with leg-of-mutton sleeves. There was Shandra, who looked like an exotic tigress. There were men in tuxedos and many women in drop-dead, entrance-making ball gowns. I saw the woman who spoke at my very first Saturday night gathering wearing a royal blue Indian sari, looking quite handsome. I was really curious about the number of attractive people. Did this consciousness make one more attractive, or what is it a prerequisite for inclusion?

However, there were diverse-looking people as well, except racially. Oddly, it seemed to be predominantly white. There were all ages, the youngest twentysomething and the oldest sixty or seventy. There were at least three men in wheelchairs.

One surprise came after another. I was recognizing people I knew, and it felt like an otherworldly reunion. It was a little shocking, as if to say "Aha, I knew you were part of this!" Everyone I had been drawn to in the last several years was in the Buddha Field. I saw Maximus, Marcus, Sapho, Creed, Aurora, Jade, and Jeff—basically everyone in my life. It was quite a gathering of all my friends, past, present, and future. Even though my excitement was overwhelming, all of our conversations were short and whispered. There was an atmosphere of deep silence, and many people were seated with eyes closed in meditation. Little did I know this would become a very small intimate family. There was open-eye meditation, beautiful music, and only hushed voices. Two women were walking around with baskets of gifts for everyone. It was a divinely enchanting room to be in.

A gorgeous buffet with salmon, turkey, roasted vegetables, sweet potatoes, and salad, all organic, was deliciously prepared by the devotees. There was one person serving every dish, making sure to have open-eye meditation with each of us, all in silence. The tables were lushly decorated with small vases of roses, bowls of oranges, and elaborately crafted name cards.

Once everyone had chosen their food and were seated, things got even quieter. At the head of the room, a table had been set on a dais with a profusion of flowers and beautiful fabrics. Thousands of red and orange rose petals were strewn to make a path to the dais. Throughout the entire room were oversized vases stuffed with orange and red roses, deep crimson dahlias, orchids, and fir branches, some five feet tall. The flowers alone rivaled any ball or wedding. I had been seated in the middle of the room at a special table for the four new people, in direct line of sight of what looked like a royal throne.

Finally, after all the years, all the thoughts, all the curiosity, all the insane longing, all the patience, all the anticipation (I was sweating and trying to meditate), he entered the room.

He was a small man, maybe five foot six inches, very fit, well-groomed, with a golden tan and short, light brown hair. It was hard to guess his age from where I was sitting in that moment. But my guess was that he was in his forties or fifties. It was also hard to determine his nationality. He was wearing a bright turquoise silk shirt and some loose pants. He slowly walked across the room and carefully took his seat. There was a piercing silence in the room. Not a word was spoken. A beautiful woman with hair past her waist, who was the only person near him, stood up, walked over, and tied a bib around his neck—like a child would wear. Then she sat, and everyone began eating their meals. We ate in silence until the same woman stood up, walked a few feet, and handed a microphone to the first person to her right.

At this point the person who received the mic put down his fork and read the message that was rolled inside the gift, one of which we had all received earlier in the evening. Each message was a quote from The Yoga Master. I was a little nervous about using the microphone and speaking to the entire room. Mine said, *"Be quiet and listen to the silence within."* Some were humorous and some had an uncanny way of applying specifically to a particular person, even though the gift bags were randomly selected.

After the mic made its way around to everyone, most had finished their dinner, and The Master finally began to speak. He addressed the group with a heavy Latino accent and spoke very deliberately yet softly, with a certain cadence to his delivery.

He gave satsang, the sharing of truth, and talked about how the highest service you could perform on the planet was to wake up. He told very good stories, as well as some X-rated jokes involving the names of some of the people in the room. He was funny, charming, mesmerizing, and intoxicating.

He used the words *mystery school*, which seemed to send a chill of authenticity through me. I had heard we were one, but it just carried a certain impact coming from him. I had read about such places but only very slightly, because there is obviously not a lot written about these schools because they descend from a long, private, ancient tradition. According to the Aquarian Gospel, Jesus attended a mystery school in the eleven years in which there is no Biblical record of his activities. Rumi talks about a mystery school, and it is well known that Sufis had them also. The concept of these ancient orders is to leave the way of the world and the self behind to merge with the "One Self." They are called schools because a master has to be present to guide you there. As The Master said, "If you want to know about God, find a teacher. If you want to become God, find a Master." This always rang true for me. Finally, I was going to be shown the way to enlightenment. To me, becoming God just meant becoming who you truly were, in the cosmic sense. I was excited.

So this is what this is. My mind now had a label. I was in a mystery school. There was no physical building. In other words, it was an ashram without walls.

This also explained why everything around The Master was so secret. No one could know that he existed. A wave of knowing ran through me. We were a select, noble, and elite collection of evolved souls worthy of protection, even though we weren't supposed to call ourselves an organization, a religion, or even a group. Identifying ourselves as people of this caliber helped me feel justified in lying to everyone in my life because, as I saw it, the mystery school was of the highest order.

During his satsang, my mind kept trying to have a transcendental experience like Lahiri Mahasaya had had with Babaji. My thoughts stopped me from fully enjoying this very charismatic man and simply being in the moment. I had read once about Master Charles, who had a transcendental experience just by staring at a photograph of his master, Muktananda. Expectations were robbing me of the moment once again. But there had been so much anticipation leading up to this, it was hard to stay present and let go of all expectations. Everyone was transfixed by his words, which seemed to carry so much more than just their literal meaning, as if there was a transmission of energy that filled the room. It's funny how I never remembered exactly what he said. I just remember the essence, which was love and consciousness. I was getting a glimpse of the state "beyond the mind."

After dinner he disappeared upstairs, trailed by a group of four male attendants.

"Oh, that's his personal entourage," said a very handsome woman wearing a royal blue ball gown. She took me by the arm. "That one is his constant companion. And that one works on his body. And those two live with him and take care of him," she continued as I got the insider's tour.

"They are all so handsome," I commented. I noticed that they looked like fashion models. I was trying to absorb all this new information that had been so forbidden up to this point.

A flood of questions arose in me. Now, he was no longer an abstract figure but a person in the flesh. Did he have a family? What was his nationality? Did he have a job? Was he married? Was he gay? Did he have children? Did he have sex? What did he do before he was a master? How did one become a master? I remembered Mara telling me when she invited me to the party, "Even though he's enlightened, he still has a personality." What did that mean, exactly?

She didn't answer but pulled me out of the way as his entourage came walking through. It was time to dance as everyone filed into the ballroom. All the tables had been cleared and put away in very short order.

A buffet of delectable desserts had been put out and was being swarmed upon as if by locusts. People were changing clothes and putting on ballroom dancing shoes. Uh-oh, this looked serious.

At this point, The Master reentered the room, and the music changed. He was wearing tight shorts, a blue tank top, and ballet shoes with thin white socks. Next, a tall, thin, blond woman, who was obviously going to be his dance partner, appeared. *Whoa*, I thought, *that is the same woman from the yoga class who Maximus had a fling with*. Who was this stunningly beautiful woman?

The woman and The Master took the floor and were fabulous. Their style was professional and flawless, and it seemed they surely had been dancing together for years. They could rumba, tango, soft shoe, waltz, salsa, you name it. It was amazing by anyone's standards, including those of *Dancing with the Stars*.

Soon after the performance, we were all invited to dance. We danced like Greeks, we line danced, and some devotees performed elegant waltzes that traveled in a big circle. Later, we all danced to rock and hip-hop. We danced all night, and I was completely swept away by the energy, the people, the music, and the ambience. I felt like Cinderella at the ball.

The Master continued to dance with the group, and everyone took special care not to bump into him. We were all aware of where he was on the dance floor at all times.

Suddenly, without any fanfare, amidst this swirl of true celebration, stillness set in. A small group had stopped and were all looking toward the center of the ballroom. Others stopped until the whole ballroom came to a standstill.

I looked in the middle of the circle and there was The Master standing in front of a woman. He was close to her but not touching her, and looking into her eyes. Then he put his fingers over her eyes to let her know she should close her eyes. Then he put his index finger in the middle of her forehead and held it there for a while, with a slight vibration.

Afraid to make a sound, I very quietly whispered to someone, "What is happening?"

"He is giving her *shakti.*" Unbeknownst to me, The Master was a giver of *shakti*, or *shaktipat,* as it is known. Shakti is divine energy, and the touch of it can activate the shakti in your own body, which is a conduit of blissful energy. Some people describe shakti as liquid love, pure consciousness, or a divine current that feels like you are being made love to. The touch of The Master delivering shakti wakes up the divine love in you.

After a few minutes, this woman got on her knees with the help of two members of his entourage, and then she bowed down. From a kneeling position, she lowered herself down and laid her upper body over her knees with her arms outstretched in front of her, forehead touching the ground. This was the first time I had seen someone bow down to The Master. After a short time, and with some assistance, she sat up and closed her eyes in meditation, remaining in that state for quite a while.

Apparently everyone in the room wanted shakti. At this point in the evening, the energy transformed from celebration to complete silence and stillness. You could hear a pin drop.

We knew we were witnessing something sacred. He continued with more people in what appeared to be a random order. Some people would place themselves in front of him in the hopes of being the next recipient.

He worked with everyone differently. Some were touched on the heart and others on the eyes. Everyone had a different response. Some were completely quiet. Some moaned as if having an orgasm. Some gasped, and some cried. Some had to be held up so as not to fall. Some quivered. Some shook and started to tremble. This was something I had never seen before.

I was actually glad that I was not picked. What if I felt nothing? Would I have to appear as if I felt something even if I didn't? I felt a touch of performance anxiety even though I truly wanted to receive a direct transmission of divine energy.

After giving shakti to about a dozen people, The Master took a seat near the front of the room as everyone gathered around him, grabbing spots on the floor and bringing up chairs. Everyone closed their eyes for a final meditation. At some point he said, "Namaste." Everyone in the room dropped to their knees to bow to The Master. Though I hesitated, I felt compelled to bow as well. And so began my life in a mystery school. He left the room as everyone stayed still for a few more moments. The ball was over.

"Well, this was an early one," Maximus said as he was driving me home. I looked at the clock, and it was four o'clock in the morning. I had been there for twelve hours, and it felt like three. It had definitely been a magical evening, like riding on a wave that just kept getting higher and higher.

The next morning I felt like I had a hangover, although there was no alcohol at the celebration. Maybe it was the hours and hours of dancing. I did notice that I did not feel like talking. An old, distantly familiar, and very deep silence had descended on me. I got a call from Jade asking me to lunch at Mr. Natural, a local vegetarian restaurant on the east side. He said there were some people from the party going, and it would be good if I could come. I accepted because I felt like I should. It turned out to be a big mistake.

At lunch with about ten people, I was asked several questions: "What did you think?" "What was your experience?" and "Can you share what happened, Janis?" I was not ready for this, and I was a little angry with myself for not honoring the profound silence I had entered. I had compromised myself for a "should." I quickly gathered my things and left, which actually created even more questions later.

I learned that sharing or expressing your experience was a valued and important part of this whole process. There was an unspoken code of ethics involved. First, it is good to share. You spoke only of your experience, not something you read in a book and not someone else's experience. There was a whole language that went along with it. If it was sincere and beautiful, you would be in the vibration of truth. Speaking insincerely, you could sound like a parroting of Buddha Field language. The Buddha Field had its own lingo, which sounded strange at first but was so commonly used that one picked it up practically by osmosis. Here is a glossary of some of the common terms:

Spending time with: Dating or seeing someone; being romantically involved or in a sexual relationship with.

Conscious company or *Holy company*: People in the Buddha Field.

Going all the way: Reaching enlightenment.

Getting guidance: Asking significant questions about your life such as what to do involving your love life, whether or not to travel, who to sleep with or not, who to spend time with, what to do about your job, or your family—basically, about anything and everything. It was a sign of maturity that you asked for guidance from The Master, because that meant that you were serious about going all the way. It was a privilege to be able to ask for guidance. However, even if you asked for guidance, you were not guaranteed to receive it.

I was gone: Blissed out or intoxicated by God.

The body: Used instead of "my body."

Drop your body: To die.

I am soooooo grateful: Something said often and not always sincerely.

Follow guidance: This meant doing what The Master suggested.

Deluded: This meant that you did what you wanted to do and didn't follow guidance; gone astray; way overused by members of the Buddha Field, often as a cover-up for judgment.

I was in my mind: It was your ego operating, not the real you.

Drop your mind. To stop identifying with an experience or a person. This meant to drop into meditation and stop identifying with the false ego; to stop feeling what you are feeling and rise above it; to transcend the ego or any emotions you were having. (This often felt very harsh when you heard it from someone, and was usually impossible to accomplish.)

Service: The work you were assigned to do, which, of course, was a privilege and to be done as an honor or an offering; to give yourself selflessly.

I could barely understand the voice on the other end of the line because of the loud noises in Mr. Natural. I finally realized it was Norm, the private detective, and I quickly ran outside to get away from the noise.

"I might have gone too far," was the first thing he said. A feeling of fear coursed through me about either being found out or about what I was about to find out.

"So they all went to this church on Monday night, a Catholic one, over there off Oltorf Avenue. They got there about eight and everyone was carryin' chairs and blankets, maybe some robes again. I waited a while before I went in. When I did, I just walked right in. I didn't ask nobody for permission or nothin' like that. I figured I'd find more out that way. So I see all these people, maybe fifty of 'em, sittin' around in a circle.

"In the middle of the floor is just this tape recorder. Then some big guy comes walkin' up to me and says, 'This is a private class.' Well, I told him I was innerested, and he told me I was gonna have to leave cuz it was private. Well, I went ahead and left, 'cause it looked like he was serious. But first I went to the office of the church and asked the lady how I could join that class. She didn't know nothin' about it, but looked it up for me and then said that it was an acting class. A private acting class. They were there till way past one in the mornin'," Norman explained.

Hmmmm. A church, I thought. Here I am participating fully in this group, and there was still so much I didn't know about it and was *not invited to*. No one likes to be excluded, so this brought up all kinds of pain and misery for me. One of my deepest wounds was being ignored, which also translated into feeling left out and not feeling special. I would have to go to Jeff for some cleansing.

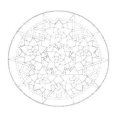

CHAPTER 15

Cinderella Goes to Class

I would have to wait to find out what "church" was about. I had become used to wanting more out of this experience, although ambition was something you were to leave at the door. This was very humbling. And maybe that was the purpose. Humility had never been one of my strong suits. I knew that humility was to "make oneself small, not proud or arrogant, unpretentious." I had read once that this quality alone could give you God realization.

I heard a story about a man who asks his master how long it would take for him to become enlightened. "Twenty more lifetimes," the master replied. The man walks away dejected. Others come to ask and get various answers. No one is satisfied. Finally the janitor walks by and the master asks if he wants to know how long it will take him. The janitor cannot believe his good fortune to even have the chance to ask. "Fifty more lifetimes," says the master. Upon hearing this, the janitor cries out in ecstasy, *"Only* fifty more lifetimes! That is wonderful!" His gratitude was so great that he was enlightened at that moment and he achieved God realization.

I was the opposite of the janitor. I had trained the survivor and the striver in me to get what I wanted either through cleverness, intelligence, doing, calculating, or sheer will. So to find a way to unlearn all this behavior, I had to wind my way back to innocence. That was my new mission, and it couldn't be from a place of ambition. This was something worth unlearning, and learning how to be vulnerable was my first step. What a realization! Enlightenment could not be obtained by approaching life in the same way I always had. I could not make it happen. The Master would later share with me how in the Bhagavad Gita, Krishna explains to Arjuna why cleverness is useless.

As time passed, I had slowly experienced a physical transformation, as were many of the people around me. Maximus and I consistently swam at Barton Springs, which I consider to be the true heart of Austin. It is a large, natural-bottom pool lined with ancient pecan and oak trees. It is a soulful gathering place. On a hot summer day you, could find a whole hillside of scantily clad university students lying on blankets, soaking up the sun and then cooling off in the springs. There were people playing the guitar, drum circles, some serious swimmers, and occasionally a few topless coeds. It was the Venice Beach of Austin. You could not leave those sacred waters without feeling refreshed, free of stress, and blissful.

But besides working out and swimming, meditating consistently for at least two hours a day physically changed me. According to some, meditation can slow or even reverse the aging process. I felt meditation was having a positive effect on how I looked and felt. People just started to look better in this "company." I remember making a mental note of how people looked when someone new came around, which was not often. And then I would slowly watch in amazement how that person would completely transform. Even the ones I considered physically unattractive would miraculously bloom and become beautiful. It was as though their skin was more luminous, their features softened, and their best physical attributes would become more pronounced. They had jewels in their eyes. It was amazing. My idea of beauty was also changing. It was less about the shell and more about the light that shone through, like a lantern. It was as if The Master could see the diamond in the rough and then know exactly how to polish it to get the maximum brilliance.

I was amazed with myself. I was in a good place mentally, physically, and emotionally. I felt free from psychological traumas, more at ease with the world, more present, and very focused on what was important: my children, my relationships, and my path to enlightenment. I felt almost bulletproof from the stresses of life. People I hadn't seen in a while would comment that they barely recognized me. But the transformation was more than skin deep. Everything about me and my life changed. I didn't do the same things, and I didn't see the same people. I kept company mainly with my children and other people in the Buddha Field. I didn't look, feel, or act the same.

One astute friend, who had no idea what I was up to, asked me, "So, who are your friends these days, and what are you doing?" I completely evaded her question. But I couldn't blame her for being curious. If I were watching this kind of a change in someone I knew, I would be asking a lot of questions too.

This path was all-consuming. I never did find out about the meeting at the church until I was invited to go to "class," which actually had nothing to do with church. It just took place at a church that was rented. The only thing I knew was that I would be making a commitment, for as long as class existed, to attend every Monday night. And of course, I was not to mention it to anyone, which was standard operating procedure.

I couldn't wait to go.

I was given directions to a church and told to bring a chair. No one knew that I already knew the address. In some ways, getting invited to class was like arriving. I was excited and slightly afraid, having no idea what would happen.

It was the middle of summer, and everyone showed up in tank tops and super-casual yoga-type clothes. People were tanned and relaxed as they filed in. It was a large group of about a hundred and twenty people. A young guy with tattoos, a tank top, and a bandana was setting up a microphone next to a folding chair in the middle of the room. The Master would be conducting class, and that would be his seat. I had not seen him since the celebration, and I wasn't aware that he was coming. This added some major horsepower to my excitement, as I had heard so many stories about his enlightening presence, as well as about his personality and how he could be really tough on devotees.

I don't really know why we were asked to commit to showing up for class, because I couldn't imagine not wanting to show up. It would turn out to be the most entertaining, hilarious, serious, terrifying, unpredictable, heartbreaking, poignant, insightful, educational, transformational, unbelievable six hours you could spend anywhere, anytime. It was human drama at its finest and most raw, led by a master acting teacher, The Master.

When everyone was completely quiet and meditating, The Master would enter the room, shuffling along in his house slippers. He usually wore baggy shorts (the same pair), white socks, his trademark slippers, and a tank top. There was always music, and for a long time it was the same ethereal piece. It was his entrance theme. I can barely hear that piece of music today without feeling a flood of emotions. Then he would take a seat and gaze at every single person in the room without saying a word—at least a hundred and twenty people—in open-eye meditation. This created immediate intimacy with every person, to connect in that way. It also seemed to transport everyone out of their daily dramas and into the focus of the present moment. He was dialing us in.

"Cloooose theee eeeeyes," were always his first words. It was a slow incantation to begin.

What followed was usually an imaginary scenario he would present to stimulate some deep feelings or insights. They could be real-life or allegorical. This was called "class exercise." Whoever wanted to share would raise his or her hand. He would take his time and choose only two or three people a night, as this process was always quite an ordeal. The person would then walk to the center of the room and take a seat in the chair facing The Master, adjust the microphone, and start speaking. You would speak about your experience of the exercise and what you had discovered.

It took so much courage to get up into the chair. For me, it was fear of public speaking to the hundredth power, because you were pouring out your soul in the most vulnerable way possible in front of a large group of peers. If you were talking about something really personal, which is what everyone did, The Master would look at you and say, "There's nobody here except you and me." And that's how you were supposed to approach it. I felt like a voyeur at times, listening to things so personal I would sometimes cringe inside. We heard about sexual abuses never before spoken, sheepish admissions of sexual inadequacies, deep sexual confusion, life-threatening illnesses, regretted abortions, criminal confessions, crippling jealousies, plots for revenge, and other dark family secrets. I was shaken to see so many grown men reduced to sobbing, gasping children. Sometimes people screamed and cried as it turned into a cleansing session. The level of "realness" went beyond where anyone had gone before, as there was no way to wear a mask, hide, or avoid the messiness of the human experience.

So much love was created among everyone, all from the sheer witnessing of everyone's extreme vulnerability. After a while, you came to a place where whoever was in the chair became you. The empathy and love was so strong, there was no room for judgment. You saw yourself in everyone's confessions and in everyone's experiences.

Many people avoided the chair as long as possible. Some loved it and were always raising their hands. Just to raise your hand was a tremendous act of bravery. I'm quite sure that everyone remembers their first time in the chair. I do.

During this period, I found myself to be all-consumed with this life. Yet I would have wild moments of self-doubt that would flare up, thinking this was all a hoax and I was completely crazy. I would think that The Master was an imposter and that we were all fools. I was getting in deep and having to make up a lot of stories about where so much of my time was being spent out of the house. I felt guilty about the children and the time I was taking away from them. After a while, the doubt drove me crazy. One day I made a decision. I was going to either get out, or trust that this was real and good. But no matter what, there would be no more doubting.

I created a test in my mind, and I was looking for signs and certainty. I desperately wanted to know that I was on the right path because I had devoted nearly every aspect of my life to the mystery school and my new master. The sign came one night as class was ending and we were all in deep meditation. I was suddenly overwhelmed with the deepest sense of profound gratitude, not only for my life, but for this experience.

As I walked out of the class that night in deep reverence, I caught a glimpse of the corner of a woman's eye. There was so much beauty in her eye, time stopped. I was instantly transported by this precious, seemingly insignificant observation. It was a moment in time that surprised me, delighted me, and offered an invitation to a level of consciousness that I never knew existed. It was another octave of awareness that instantly revealed itself. I had been looking for certainty that this path was right, and I had received my sign. I made my choice. I threw doubt out the window and decided I was "all in."

After several months, the class moved locations to a theater, where it felt like life was imitating art. I finally summoned the nerve to raise my hand a couple of times, but had not been called up to the chair yet. Finally, my lucky day arrived.

"Janis Joplin," The Master said as he called me up to the chair. I took a seat under the literal spotlight. "Take the ice cream cone," he said, directing me to pull the microphone up to my mouth. "So where is your boa?" he asked in his heavy accent.

"My bra?" I answered, thinking he said *bra*. Chuckles floated throughout the room. "Oh, my boa," I then said, understanding the Janis Joplin reference. "In my closet," I replied. He was obviously just trying to lighten things up.

"I bet you have a lot of things in your closet," he said as he peered deeply into my eyes.

"That's true, I do." I wanted to keep my comments honest and thoughtful.

After a few moments, I shared what I had seen in the exercise—a ceramic slipper my grandmother used to keep in a drawer in her dresser. I hadn't thought about it in years.

"What I see with you, Janis, is your allurement into the rebellious world, not really knowing what the true rebellion is. The true rebellion is complete surrender. All other-worldly rebellions are mostly desperate attempts at escape from the true one. I also see your identification with the Cinderella story, waiting for your prince to show up. I don't know your history, but maybe you were raised feeling like the ignored stepchild with only rags. You were just waiting for the day that Prince Charming would come and find you. But that will never happen. There is no Prince Charming except the unconditional love that is found only through true surrender. That is where true freedom lies and is the end of all rebellion."

I'm not sure what else he said, but I felt like he was looking into me. He could truly see me.

After a few moments of open-eye meditation, I bowed down, feeling a little like a debutante making a curtsy. At the same time, I felt grateful surrendering in reverence as I returned to my seat.

Another time in the chair, he looked into for my eyes for a long time. "Look over here," he finally said, holding his finger off to the right. I did. "Now look over here," he said, holding his finger to the left. He repeated this, each time bringing his finger in a little closer to his body.

After a while he said, "There. Now you are in focus. You seem to have very scattered energy, as if you have trouble focusing on one thing or giving anything your full and true attention. There is a focus to your being that has been missing." At that moment, I felt completely clear and focused in my life— maybe for the first time.

CHAPTER 16

No Name

One thing I soon learned was that The Master sometimes gave people new names. There was no formal ceremony because it was spontaneous for various people. Some people wanted a new name but never got one. Some never wanted a new name but got one anyway. When I heard about this, I started harboring a secret desire for a new name. Why not let my name reflect the new person I was becoming? Besides, I never really liked my birth name. We never get a choice in our birth names. Soon I spread it around that I was open to a new name.

I realized that it was not so much the new name that holds a new vibration. Rather, The Master gives a name that has a vibration more conducive and in alignment with your true self and who you are becoming. That sounded good to me.

The next week The Master started calling me Mercedes. That was OK with me, and I liked the name. But he never formally indicated that it was my new name. He just called me Mercedes and I wondered why. Was he referring to Mercedes, the car, or was it the Mexican songstress named Mercedes, who we had recently seen perform? Regardless, I liked it.

"So does that mean that's my new name?" I asked a girl-friend.

I polled around and got a lot of opinions. The answer I got was "Yeah, for sure. Just start using it." That was all I needed to hear.

At the time, I was teaching yoga, and I couldn't wait to change my name on the schedule and announce my new name. As part of a long yogic tradition, it was not uncommon to be given a name by your guru. I had no idea what to say when asked about this new name since I could not say that I had a master or a teacher. I would make up something. Creating explanations would turn out to be a very good skill. I changed my name to Mercedes.

One night during class and out of the blue, The Master looked at me and said, "Mercedes is not your name. Why are you using it?" Fear, sweat, adrenaline, and complete humiliation washed over me as all eyes were looking at me. I felt judged, embarrassed, and ashamed for being so presumptuous.

"I never said that was your name. I think I will call you La Toya from now on." And that was that. I was now La Toya.

Luckily, no one outside the Buddha Field had really paid too much attention to me when I asked them to start calling me Mercedes, only those friends in the Buddha Field. Nobody really called me La Toya except The Master.

More time passed. I should have known this was not over. He had a way of taking a theme, such as my identification with my image, and really working with you on it. I thought La Toya was an insulting name, maybe after La Toya Jackson, who might be perceived as shallow, tacky, and without class: a poser. It made me uncomfortable to think that maybe these qualities applied to me, but I was not afraid to look at that. Mercedes seemed like a much more elegant label. He was a genius at getting to your core issue and working like a surgeon to cut away those parts that were no longer needed. Most of the time he performed the surgery with no anesthesia. The pain could be deep, but transformational as well. My next "name" encounter would turn out to be my "bring down the house" chair experience. We were at the theater. I was not in the chair. I was just a face in the crowd.

"Who would like a new name?" he announced to the group one evening.

Namings were rare, and group namings were extremely rare, if they had ever occurred at all. Not only that, but being asked if you wanted a name was even more rare. Everyone's attention was on point, to say the least.

I threw my hand up. Even though I had been given two names, I did not want to end up with LaToya. Who could take that name seriously?

He didn't call on me. He first called on one of his senior disciples, Tom. They had been together about sixteen years, probably more. The Master took his time with Tom, deservedly so. After trying on several names, he was given Nick, short for Nicholas. It was a tender and sweet interchange between two men who seemed to have been traveling together on an inner journey for a long time.

"Who else wants a new name?" he said again, and quite a few hands shot up.

"LaToya, what about you? Are you still wanting a new name?" he said, seeming to rub it in about my hungry image desire and my need to feel special.

"Yes," I boldly declared.

"Are you ready to be grateful for what is given and become a nobody?"

"Yes," I repeated.

"Well, let's see. For you I see maybe something like, hmmmmm, Malena. She was a well-known Greek singer. What do you think about that?"

First of all, I had never heard of her. Secondly, I didn't like the name. "I don't really like it," I sheepishly replied. A hush consumed the room. I could just imagine everyone thinking how ungrateful I was to turn down the rare gift of a name. The Master paused and glared at me. I was mortified.

"Well, who else would like the beautiful name Malena?" Hands shot up. "What about you, Maria? Would you like that name? It would fit you very well." It was true. Maria had striking features and could pass for Greek.

"Yes, Master," she said, and blushed. She would take it and was grateful for it. Then he turned back to me and glared again. I was starting to feel a little like an ungrateful child being admonished in front of her friends. "Okay, LaToya. I'm going to give you one more chance. Hmmmmm. Let's see. What about Meleessa?" he asked. *Eeeeeeeeew*, I thought. I really didn't like this name either. I disliked it even more than Malena. It reminded me of someone I knew in college who I didn't really like. *Meleessa* felt mousy and weak.

"Welllll?" he asked. The whole crowd was holding their breath waiting for my response.

"I don't really like it." I grimaced as I said it, knowing that it was probably not the favorable answer. I just could not surrender. I had this idea in my mind of wanting a name I could be proud and fond of, and I just didn't want to settle. Was it stubbornness, an inability to surrender, a desperation to rise beyond my origin? Or was it the fear of being trapped in mediocrity forever? Added to this was my tendency to disregard and fight authority. Regardless, The Master was pushing all my buttons at this moment, the main one being having a name that elevated me and not demeaned me. The crowd gasped in absolute disbelief at the audacity of my ungratefulness and began to murmur about my unwillingness to "be a yes" to The Master. I thought, at this moment, there was a good chance I could be ousted forever.

"WHAT? WHAT DO YOU MEAN?" he screamed. His voice was getting louder and stronger, like I had never heard it before. Perhaps I had pushed a button in him. By this time, the energy in the room was on tilt, and things were very uncomfortable. I started to sweat.

In desperation, I turned to Marco, a senior disciple who was sitting to my left. I desperately whispered to him, "Do I have to say yes, even if I don't like the name?"

Marco said with the utmost earnestness, "This is between you and your Master."

For some reason, this empowered me to stand even more strongly in my resolve, though I knew this was an exercise in surrender.

"That's right. I just don't like it," I firmly blurted out. There was a long pause as the crowd groaned in disgust and disbelief.

"YOU HAVE A VERY BIG EGO, MY DEAR, VERY BIG. FROM NOW ON I AM GOING TO CALL YOU 'NO NAME.' " And he did. That was my new name. He used it, and those brave enough used it too. So my lesson was a big, steaming hot serving of humble pie. I accepted this humility and this new name, or lack thereof, gracefully.

After class as everyone was leaving, people could hardly look at me. I was wearing the scarlet letter. The only consolation was my friend Jade, who came up to me.

He said, "Well, one time I almost did something as bad as that. I stood up in class and demanded that The Master give me the direct experience of God right there, and the whole room, including him, went crazy on me." At least one person was still talking to me.

After this epic clash, I was not kicked out. However, people took my new name to heart. I was called No Name by everyone in the group for the next year and a half. I felt like there might be a hidden gem in this harsh teaching. Maybe every time someone referred to me as No Name, the preoccupation I had with image would be transmuted into something higher. I was willing to learn and accept. One part of me was grateful for this teaching.

Eventually I would learn that the direct experience of God was what we all wanted. But as it was told to me, it would never be on OUR terms. The road was narrow. Many tried, but few succeeded. The qualities needed were humility, surrender, service, a willingness to be a nobody, and a "yes" to The Master, as well as complete gratitude for whatever was given. I knew that it wasn't going to be easy. I didn't consider myself much of a servant to anyone or anything, and I had always questioned authority. With The Master, I wanted to say no, and then he could decide what needed to be done with that part of me. It wasn't out of lack of respect. I was just being authentic and true to my nature.

Another aspect of class was the group exercises. Small groups would stand up to participate in an endless variety of exercises that were designed to give you insight and experiential teachings. After, we would sit and share our experiences. There were so many over the years. They could make a whole book.

One in particular happened after 9/11. Some chairs were set up to mimic the inside of an airplane. People sat in the chairs. Several were playing the role of terrorists or hijackers. We reenacted getting hijacked. When I say reenacted, I mean people actually were getting hijacked emotionally. We played with no rules, except there would be no bodily harm. We had some very strong and powerful men and women in the group. It was beyond acting. The experience was intensely physical and emotional, with people pinned to the ground, terrorized and physically harassed and screamed at. It was as wild as your imagination could go. Many times, the goal was to see what insight this brought up for people and also to practice remaining in meditation while under extreme situations. Surprisingly, I found myself not fearful, but calm and wanting to help calm those around me. In severely stressful situations, I usually became calm. This was similar to when my father asked me as a teen what to do about his affair. The hero in the family (me) would rise to the occasion.

There were layers of teaching to each exercise. This particular exercise was an analogy of how we get hijacked every day, every moment, by our minds and our thoughts. I realized how much my thoughts were focused on my insecurities, including whether my boyfriend liked me, how I looked physically, needless worry, shopping, to-do lists and more.

Other exercises were fun, but most were very confronting to the ego.

"No Name, stand up," The Master said one evening. I did. "Sing us an opera," he instructed. "In German," he added. He might as well have said, "Take off all your clothes on national television with really bad lighting." The truth is, I cannot sing, not to mention I don't know German. I was not even allowed to be in the sixth-grade choir. That's how badly I sing. And in front of this entire room? I became a tornado of fear and adrenaline as I walked out to the center of the room, with all two hundred and forty eyes and a spotlight on me.

You couldn't escape by making a joke of it and trying to look more stupid than you already looked. It had to be a genuine effort.

Obviously, I had no choice but to fake the German. And I would make it sound like a lullaby because I knew some sweet melodies I sang to my children. I opened my mouth and gave my best attempt at singing an operatic lullaby in German.

It wasn't good. My voice was squeaky, not loud enough, off tone, off everything. But I was sincerely trying to make my voice hauntingly beautiful and sweet. After I was done, I sat down. No one said a word. Someone else was called up.

After that, and all the countless times things like this happened, I don't think there is much in life that would scare me or humiliate me in front of a group. At the time I didn't realize what a powerful teaching this was—to be humiliated and then to witness the humiliation of others. I realized that humiliation was a collective experience. Compassion for those who are humiliated is to truly see oneself in others.—and then finally to come to a place where you can ask yourself, "Who is feeling humiliated?" And the "who" is always my smaller self, identifying with some aspect of the child or the ego. Who I really am cannot be humiliated. This teaching gave me freedom from the fear of looking stupid. I had never really known that the fear of looking stupid was so strong in me. Growing up, looking stupid translated to even less attention from my father.

Sometimes, right in the middle of a serious group exercise, The Master would spontaneously announce "Fruit salad!" That was the cue for a game where everyone would stand up, run around, change places, scream and shout, and basically go crazy. Complete pandemonium would break out, and we were like kindergarteners released for recess. Everyone would come together to laugh at the chaotic exercise. It felt like we were also recognizing the absurdity of life in general. The Master was like a cosmic director yelling "Cut!" to all the seriousness and illusions of *maya*, the Sanskrit word for the physical world of space and time.

It seemed all of us were palpably excited to congregate at any gathering, especially at the theater, where I had the opportunity to see all of my friends in a public space. I always tried to look my best, even though I pretended not to care. I was still grappling with my journey, which was so much about letting go of the importance of my image. As the group gathered, there was always a buzz in the air like that of an old-world gypsy market, with people peddling their wares and services, or promoting a cause—raw food or kombucha tea, making announcements, campaigning for volunteers, gossiping, primping, collecting money for class, checking everyone else out, lounging around, lying on the floor giving chiropractic adjustments, giving one another massages—there were no rules, just instincts. And there was fierce competition for seating positions as everyone tried to be as close to The Master as possible. Competition was a large part of this experience; even though we were supposed to be beyond that with our brothers and sisters in the group, a hierarchy was definitely in place. During Halloween, some members produced a skit about the vicious battling for seating every week. Nick once playfully called it the "den of thieves."

There was so much love for all the brothers and sisters who participated in one another's growth during these classes. The things we saw each other birth, exorcise, confess, confront, expose, admit, surrender, release, and transform into were phenomenal. There are no words for the compassion they stirred. The entire class witnessed a woman taken through an extremely personal cleansing involving her never-spoken-about incestuous childhood molestation. But sometimes, it wasn't about reliving a traumatic experience. Simply being confronted with raw truth was serious enough. I saw an actor strip himself bare (figuratively) and melt into a raw pulp of insecurity and complete vulnerability after an intense line of questioning by The Master. I saw long-dead relationships healed between enemies as psychic swords were laid down in the name of love.

We practiced our deaths, and we relived our births. We screamed in a primal way until we were sobbing blobs lying in puddles on the floor. We innocently and passionately kissed people we would never in a million years dream of kissing.

We danced constantly. We sang our hearts out every single class. We exposed our Achilles' heels to everyone. And if we didn't, they were exposed for us. We volunteered for the messy surgical removal of those aspects of ourselves no longer serving the highest good. We constantly cried, witnessing each other, and we always managed to laugh. I have often said that the bonds of friendship and closeness forged in these classes would never be experienced again in this lifetime with that level of intensity. I tried to explain that to my boyfriend years later. Unfortunately, he would never be able to understand.

After these classes, every play, theater performance, and television show paled in comparison to the depth of these pure and potent human dramas. No live entertainment could ever touch this.

I had been avoiding Norman's phone calls for a while. I just didn't want to have to meet him to terminate our secret business relationship. I used to jump at the chance to find out more things I wasn't supposed to know. But now I was on the inside. I was one of the people he was now watching. I didn't need him anymore, and I wanted to sever ties with Norman before it went any further. No one knew I had hired him, and his work had gotten me through some unbearable curiosities of the ego. But now, I had forged trusting bonds with people, and I couldn't betray that. I didn't want someone from the outside looking in. But we would have to have one last meeting.

"Well, I know where the headquarters is for the whole operation, I think." Norman was eager to share his latest data with me.

"It's over, Norman. I'm not seeing my boyfriend, and I don't care anymore," I said. It wasn't true, but how could I tell him I had joined the mysterious group that I had once been so desperate to understand? Things needed to end right there and they did. Norman had fulfilled his duties, no harm was done, and we arranged a final meeting for payment. I had graduated from "let's find out the secret" to "I'll do anything to protect it."

CHAPTER 17

Shakti

One day I sent a letter to The Master asking for guidance in my relationship with Maximus. I was feeling insecure and unworthy, and I feared he would abandon me at any moment. That evening, while at a gathering, The Master didn't miss a beat and opened the evening with, "No Name, so what's this about you and Maximus breaking up?" I turned red with embarrassment and denied it.

Instead of calling me on my insecurity, which was already exposed, he shared with everyone how silly it is to see relationships as "on" or "off." He explained that you can't break up even if you wanted to, because there was already a connection between us. He further explained that once you are in relationship, you are always relating, no matter what the focus might be at any given moment. Sometimes, the relating is sweet. But sometimes, it may be painful. There is always a power struggle where one person says *yes* and the other says *no*. Confusion depends on when those sentiments switch back and forth. The Master said, "Don't be a *no* or a *yes*, but be in meditation. There is never any walking away from someone." At that moment, I experienced a shift in my desire to keep something in definable terms, to just relaxing into a flow with the world around me.

"Find the love that doesn't come or go," The Master said. He wanted us to create a more expanded view of being in any relationship. The evening took a turn when The Master called Jacob up to join him. He walked up and was asked to kneel before The Master. A hush filled the room. It was shakti time. Everyone dropped in to meditation as The Master chose various people for this privilege. After about five people, he pointed to me. A flame rose in my spine. Me? It was hard to see if he was really pointing at me because the lighting was dim. Then I realized, *Yes, he is pointing to me.*

I walked down to the stage floor of the theater, my heart racing. As excited as I was to finally have the touch of shakti, I felt anxious. My thoughts began to spin through me. I asked myself, *What if I don't do it right?* and *What if I don't feel it?* But in the middle of my raging internal dialogue, The Master asked me to stand. We stood very closely to one another and connected through our eyes. I felt like I was disappearing into him.

"Close your eyes and surrender to me," he whispered softly in my ear.

I closed my eyes as he put his hand over my heart. My breathing slowed, and my heart pounded. Suddenly, warm currents of energy began to pulse through my body. The feeling was a delicious, slow-moving nectar of love. There was a rhythm to the currents coursing through my entire being. Then I experienced an inner spasm that went from inside my body to the surface of my skin.

Next, The Master moved his hand to my forehead. As if lighting a flame, the energy shot from the base of my spine up through the middle of my forehead where his finger was touching. A new channel in me had been opened.

There would be many times over the years when I would receive shakti. It was always different. Some aspects were the same, but I usually felt an intense quaking energy at the base of my spine that would cause the rest of my body to shake. It was more than a quiver or a tremble—it was like a strong, ecstatic spasm that shook me from head to toe. Sometimes, my heart center would open so wide it felt like I was being ripped or torn open. Physically, I would literally almost be stretched in a backbend. But there was always someone there who was holding out a helping hand to prevent me from falling.

Each time I received shakti, I felt recalibrated. Just as a mechanic would recalibrate the timing of a car engine, I felt my soul was being shaken and realigned into its proper position. The new calibration seemed to bring me more in tune with myself. I was falling back into my original true nature—my authentic self. It felt so relaxing to be aligned with the divinity within. Sometimes this new calibration would feel like a new frequency or vibration that revealed a newer, richer, deeper, thicker, fuller, more resonant version of myself.

"Bring your bathing suit, pack some food, and be ready in an hour." The voice on the other end of the telephone line was exuberant. It was a beautiful warm summer day, and the entire group—all one hundred and twenty of us—was going on a Sunday afternoon outing.

I fretted a little about what to bring because I had no idea what to expect, as usual. Everyone seemed giddy with excitement, and I was asked several times if this was my first outing.

"Yes," I said. I was giddy and I could tell they knew something that I didn't. It always seemed to be that way.

Who you rode with seemed to be quite important. I was invited to ride with Maximus, so I knew I would be taken care of. I say this because there could be a lot of physical demands that I knew he would be prepared for. Maybe there would be long hours, food requirements, chairs to sit in, and even more physical considerations I couldn't imagine. So we set off with our coolers full of Tupperware containers, folding chairs, blankets, towels, and water.

I have to laugh about the Tupperware. This group was addicted to it. The Tupperware School of Enlightenment, we joked. Everyone was so busy, you just always made sure you had a meal or two with you at all times. It seemed like no one stopped for a meal; you just ate as you went. There was even a service of cooks who provided meals for a small fee, once a week. Your name was written in Sharpie across the top, so that your Tupperware always got recycled back to you. It was a telltale sign of Buddha Field membership if you lived out of Tupperware. And at Christmas, guess what you got? A Tupperware container full of treats like carob nuggets, air-popped popcorn, cookies and more—all made with no sugar, of course.

So off we went in a convoy through the Texas hill country. After driving for about an hour, we entered a park near Lake Travis, a large body of water west of Austin. We drove inside the park and now had to find the others. You wouldn't think it would be hard to spot one hundred and twenty people, but it actually was. Apparently, the site selection was driven by the need for privacy, and privacy was hard to find. We eventually found the others in a remote cove.

There were many cars strewn along a hillside. Everyone dropped off their chairs in a clearing near the water. Then we set off for a silent hike, following The Master as though he was the Pied Piper himself. The voyeur in me couldn't help but check out everyone in their bathing suits, including The Master. I reveled in the human experience of it all. I was surprised by how many men wore Speedos, including The Master. I got a lot more information than I needed about some of my brothers.

After the hike, everyone shed their shoes near the shore of the lake and entered the chilly water. Most of us went for a quarter-mile swim. Some older and physically challenged disciples stayed on shore. But the rest of us swam in unison and in complete silence. Many people brought their snorkels or goggles, and we swam out to the middle of the lake like a school of dolphins. Then we circled back and stood up in chest-high waters. We all turned our bodies to face The Master in the middle of the circle. He slowly floated up to some people and motioned for them to lie on their backs in the water. Three or four people then gathered around the person and gently put their hands underneath for support. The Master then put his hand on one's forehead and gave shakti. After it was given, the person would just float for a while, assisted by the loving hands of people supporting him.

I always tried to figure out who was going to get shakti and who wasn't. But it was pointless. No one ever knew how he made his selections. Someone once told me that he could see energy and give what was needed in the moment to help someone open up to love.

After about seven or eight people, The Master floated up to me. I slowly laid back and let others support my body. The silence became louder as my ears went underwater, and he put his hand on my forehead. The electrical currents began coursing through my body and seemed to echo within me. I could hear only my own breathing and heartbeat. I felt waves of pure divine energy running through me in rhythmic crescendos. I was quaking with energy. I started to shake, partly from the cold water, but mostly from what was flowing through me. My thoughts disappeared as I floated in pure blissful energy. I stayed supported for quite a while. After I stopped floating, I became a helper for another.

After what felt like a long period of time and many shakti deliveries, I noticed everyone had moved in closer to one another. Many of them had linked arms. We were one being embracing itself as we were united in unconditional love. The pool in which we were standing had become a pool of shakti, magically electric with the vibration of love beyond words.

After leaving the water for what seemed like hours, we all scampered to the woods to change into warm clothing and then returned to our chairs. This celebration of love was experienced through discussion and the sharing of satsang. The Master threw berries, tangerines, and other treats at us, and we all laughed like children. We were all so high, we didn't even look the same. I felt completely transformed as I looked around in awe at how incredibly beautiful these brothers and sisters were at that moment. The colors of the sunset appeared more vivid than I had ever seen as we began to ecstatically sing. That was my first of several more outings to come.

There were times when the shakti would transport me into a deep place of silence for days afterward. Until I started finding this place on my own, I was always very protective of it. While in this space, there was no need to speak or to do anything. There was just a holy vibration to which I was attuned that was so delicious, I guarded it fiercely. I would isolate myself from others so they wouldn't take me out of my sacred well of silence. This place was the seat of wisdom where nothing needed to be said.

"One who knows, speaks not; one who speaks, knows not." —*Lao Tzu, Tao Te Ching*

This state of grace comes and goes these days. I am infinitely grateful whenever it returns, for however long or short a period.

There were other times when the shakti was a current of ecstatic energy in my spine. In yoga, I was beginning to experience an intense exploding energy at the base of my spine, coursing along my spinal column while I was doing backbends.

One of my most intense shakti experiences occurred later in The Master's private garden. I knelt before The Master as he put his finger on my forehead for what seemed like a very long time. Every time I felt like I could no longer remain upright from the force of the waves of energy, he would just pour on more. I must have been very receptive that day because it just kept coming, stronger and stronger, more and more. The electrical current was high voltage, and I surrendered. After he was done and I *pranamed*, I immediately sat to meditate. It was not even within my frame of reference to get up and continue my day. I had been knocked into another dimension where time did not exist. I had the distinct feeling that if I were an instrument, a whole new set of higher and lower octaves were opened in me that I never knew I had. I entered into a deeper vibration, one I had never experienced before. I was expanded and peaceful beyond words. I was experiencing life in a completely new context.

When thoughts arose, I inevitably began considering the idea that I never wanted to leave this state of being. Then, like magic, I would dissolve back into the state of no thought. I sat there for a long time, but was eventually moved to a comfortable chair inside the house by someone else. Finally, when I opened my eyes, it was five o'clock in the afternoon. I had disappeared for five hours and returned, transformed once again, without a need to speak a word. It's hard to put into words exactly how I felt, but it was like being transported to a higher dimension, one closer to heaven where one floated on a sea of deep contentment and bliss, where love and appreciation for all there is was the only current running through me.

Watching other people receive shakti was not really supposed to be a form of entertainment, but it could be. The sport of shakti watching! I say this because sometimes people were very dramatic. I tried hard not to judge but the various moans, groans, and writhing were quite impressive.

The most off-the-chart shakti I witnessed occurred also in the garden one day. A senior disciple, who had been around from the beginning, was bringing The Master's lunch. She set down the cooler—Tupperware of course—as he began to give her shakti. She cried out in ecstasy, fell to the ground, and rolled in the grass. Then she started laughing hysterically. She laughed and laughed as if she would never stop. Then she sat in meditation, with grass all through her hair and on her face, in a sublime state of *samadhi* for a long period of time. As crazy as it seemed, I truly felt it was a genuine experience for her. For years I had been hearing Maximus play a song on his guitar that he had written, called "The Master's Touch." I finally knew what he had been singing about.

But occasionally, I still had periods of doubt. This was usually sparked by the disgruntled, uninvited partner of someone who was in the group. These people would spread rumors saying that our beloved mystery school was a cult. But how could it be a cult? No one was forcing me to come. I was free to be with my family and live my dual life. I had never looked or felt better, and my relationships were the best they had ever been. I thought cults destroyed lives, spread lies, and called people to do crazy, harmful things. No, this was no cult. But the seed of doubt had always been there.

From the outside, it would seem as though The Master had a very easy life. All of his meals were cooked, his house and gardens were completely tended to, he didn't have to drive himself anywhere, and he certainly didn't do laundry. I found it comical that as a woman who sought freedom, I was back to serving the male in the house. But "through surrender, freedom is found," I was told. So I did not question what was required. And I was getting good at that. I was glad to do whatever The Master asked and was surprised at how service would take me out of my small-mindedness. Then, after a shakti experience like the one in the garden, my doubt would dissolve. My transcendental experiences were real.

I was in deep and having to make up a lot of stories about where so much of my time was being spent out of the house. My family thought I was teaching a lot of yoga classes. My friends didn't notice, because at this point I spent time only with people in the Buddha Field. I felt guilty about the children and the time I was taking away from them. Whenever I would speak to someone in the Buddha Field about this, the answer I always got was, "Serve the highest and all will be taken care of." And I was sharing my experience with my children through my improved state of mind and my renewed energy. I came home with a clear and loving heart, able to give them so much more of myself. They were still very young and didn't really know what was going on. When I was gone, they were always under the excellent care of our beloved housekeeper, Mariela. I spent a lot of time worrying about the days the outings and meetings fell on, hoping they would coincide with the days that the children were with their father. We shared joint custody, and they were with their dad every other week. Not many people in the Buddha Field had children. But I sought advice from the people who were parents. I asked why there weren't many people with children in the Buddha Field, and the answer was that it was a hard path to walk, being able to devote so much time to service and still find a way to take care of your children. This was true.

"You are serving the highest every time you choose liberation. There is no better way to serve your children than to wake up yourself." This is what Mara frequently told me. At this point in my life, "waking up" meant becoming free from the mind that controls our thoughts and actions. It was the liberation from the ego.

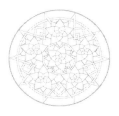

CHAPTER 18

Service

Every spiritual tradition expresses the value of selfless service. This mystery school was no exception. Since the very beginning, I was asked what I liked to do as service.

"Do you like to cook?" Sheila asked me before I had even met The Master. *God no*, I thought. In fact, I thought I would be *made* to cook, since I was so resistant to it. However, being in service did not mean being punished. You were usually given a service that you resonated with and with which you had some talent or natural affinity.

"What about cleaning?" I was asked. *Oh God, this is going to be punishment after all*, I thought.

"I teach yoga," I offered.

"Well, that is actually your job in the world," I was told. "That is not something considered to be selfless service." It was explained to me that one does not perform service work for money.

At that point I decided to offer to cook. It is interesting to think back now on how service meant only serving The Master, not the larger world, the less fortunate, or the planet. But I was completely seduced by the larger concept of being of service and knew that to become awake and selfless was of the highest order. I still did not entertain the thought that serving another human being to this extent was at all out of the ordinary. I did not feel manipulated. At the time, I felt I had purpose. And besides, we were constantly reminded that the greatest service we could perform for the planet was to wake ourselves up. I still believe that to this day.

So every Saturday morning, I would go to someone's house and help cook for The Master. Every single meal he ate was prepared by a chosen devotee. It was a beautiful service in that there was mostly silence and harmony among five people very consciously preparing his meals. I found that I actually enjoyed doing my part and not having to be the one in charge. It was fun. It took me out of my mind and into the vibration of giving selflessly, which is something extremely important for the ego to learn. Through the years I performed many different services. Each one taught me something about dropping any ideas about who I was or what I should be doing. I *really* had to drop the idea of how ironic the situation was: leaving the housework of my own home for my housekeeper while I went to do the housework for The Master. I was enjoying my experience of having a deeply devotional practice in the tradition of bhakti yoga.

Then there was the service of cleaning bird poop for years. It took me a while to graduate to that service, but here's how it began....

CHAPTER 19

The Garden

S he was a golden hippie sun goddess with her deep tan, tie-dyed bathing suit top, and long, blond, wavy hair.

"Welcome. I'm so glad you're here. This is where it all began for me and my practice really deepened," said Matilda.

It was my first day at the garden. It took quite a while, at least two years, to receive an invitation to do service in the garden. Just arriving had been quite an ordeal. I was to park at a nearby shopping center, in front of Randall's grocery store, and get into someone else's car. At least four devotees were required to ride together to reduce the number of cars showing up on a daily basis. Then we drove through a typical South Austin suburban neighborhood and arrived at a community pool with tennis courts. Behind this community center was a large section of thick woods with a creek running through it. It was actually a rare piece of raw land that had not been subdivided, obviously because of the wet-weather creek.

Then there was a walk through the woods, past a creek that actually served as a place to leave the world behind and prepare to enter sacred ground. We usually walked in silence, always, like pack mules, carrying a lot of stuff. Coming through the back way, we entered by a chicken coop and a large aviary. The aviary housed swans, ducks, peacocks, and other birds. There was a small pond with a bridge in the middle. It was a very idyllic setting. However, swans were deceptively mean, and they scared me. They tried to bite people all the time. And sometimes they succeeded.

In the center of the garden was another pond with a small waterfall. There were lily pads, and it seemed like a lotus flower was always in bloom on the water. At the top of the water-fall that cascaded down into this pool was a bronze statue of Krishna playing his flute. If you spent a lot of time around this pool, you noticed a red dragonfly that was always hovering over the lily pads and the goldfish. There were benches, and a seat hung from a tree nearby.

Also on the grounds were two organic vegetable garden beds, taken care of by several expert organic gardeners and the regular consistent help of dozens of devotees doing service.

I can remember walking into the vegetable garden in the morning when it was my service to water. I would go around and pick one leaf from every type of green growing, and there were at least a dozen. I would lay the big leaves on top of each other like a stack of paper, adding samples of all the herbs on top. Then I would tightly roll it all up like a burrito and call it an amino taco and eat it. Breakfast.

There were devotional statues everywhere: Krishna, Jesus, Mary, St. Francis of Assisi, Quan Yin, Buddha, goddesses, and angels. There were crystals hanging from the trees, wind chimes of all types constantly making their songs, as well as the desperately operatic cries of peacocks. There were paths and benches. There were some spectacular specimens of fruit trees. There was one pear tree that yielded truckloads of pears every year. There were rose bushes and rose vines and flowers every-where. Each spring there would be a huge "service" day, and many devotees would come with do-rags on their heads and help plant the spring flowers.

Close to the house was a smaller aviary with at least fifty parakeets, cockatiels, canaries, and lovebirds. This would be my service for years: cleaning out the bird poop in the small aviary. I became quite fond of all those birds as they sat on my head and pooped on my clothes over the years. People became attached to all the animals as they were all lovingly named, well cared for, and tended to. All the animals were like The Master's children.

In the morning after service was completed, The Master would usually come out of the house. I was shocked to learn right before coming to the garden that this was actually his residence. Wow. It took a long time to learn that he actually lived in Austin. I wondered for how long. He would slowly walk out the back door onto the porch, usually wearing just a pair of white briefs. Then he would engage with us as we finished our service. It was always different. Sometimes he guided us on a walk to see the beauty of what was blooming in the moment or which animals had been born or recently died. Or maybe there was a snake we were trying to catch. Usually we did tai chi with him in the morning sun. Later, we did ballet exercises, although the grass was not very conducive to this. We never went in the house, as that was for devotees who did service directly for him. I secretly harbored a desire to have a service inside the house. For one thing, I didn't like all the sun exposure, especially in the hot Texas one-hundred-degree weather. I wasn't really the "get all sweaty with outdoor work" type of girl. This was another idea I had to drop.

Bonds were formed and tested in the car rides back and forth to the house. Usually we were reminders for each other that we were serving the highest by doing this work. Many times there were conflicts, as people had other obligations like jobs. These got shoved aside in order to do service, which took hours. Personality conflicts definitely came up between the boss types and the "I don't want a boss" types. I was definitely the "I don't want a boss" type.

Something always happened in the garden. Matilda was right. It was a place where many teachings happened. Satsang was shared by The Master, and shakti was given. I loved creating a mandala almost every week. A mandala is an artistic representation of the cosmos, made up of concentric circles. In Jungian psychology, they represent an effort to reunify the self. There was a patch of brown dirt in front of the porch that served as my canvas. I usually brought roses and other flowers and delicately opened them up fully with my fingers. Then I arranged them in elaborate patterns, each one a fully fleshed-out circular mandala that would last only for a few days. Sometimes I would bring a large pile of fresh snow-cone ice for a pristine background on which to put bloodred rose petals. I would also arrange petals on The Master's walking path. I was so melted into the bhakti yoga, the practice of love and devotion, that I wrote a letter to The Master that said, *"I have found my true service. It is putting rose petals in your path. Period."*

That was all I wanted to do. One of the householders started photographing these mandalas. Someone else wanted to use the photos to create some handbags with the images printed on them. I would completely get lost in the creation of these mandalas. Everyone thought I was selflessly doing this service that I created, but actually it was selfish, because every time I sat on that bucket and started creating, I slipped into an ecstatic no-mind place. I thought, *Well, that cannot happen every time.* But it did. When someone came up and wanted to help, it was very hard for me to let someone else into my magical paradise. Having constant access to that place of intoxicating beauty was habit-forming.

In this divine romance, this was my period of falling, falling, falling in love. I have a photo of myself, taken by my daughter, of me sitting at our kitchen table as I am drawing roses. The LOOK in my eyes says it all: "I am gone in love."

It was also at this point where these moments of intoxicating beauty turned a corner. They were now moments of excruciating beauty. The only way I could describe being arrested by beauty to such a degree was that I felt like something was squeezing my heart so tightly that love dripped out.

The first time it happened, I was standing at the kitchen sink at home. I turned on the water and, as it was coming out, it became so beautiful—it was a stream of white diamonds with infinite facets and sparkles. It took my breath away. It was like a wellspring of light, the life force of beauty itself, pouring forth from my kitchen faucet.

I was transfigured by these experiences. Once again, it was like entering a higher dimension in slow motion, where time stood still. It was more like heaven where everything was holier, brighter, and saturated in light and love.

"No Name." I heard The Master call my name as he came out of the house one day in the garden. He walked over to the small aviary and was looking for me. He stopped right in front of me, very close, eye to eye.

"You have been No Name long enough. Do you like the name Giselle?" he asked. "Giselle?" I repeated.

"Yes, Giselle," he said. "From the ballet *Giselle*," he added.

The exchange was so fast, I was a little in shock. I didn't expect that this would even come up again after being called No Name for almost two years. I believed the name *Giselle* was way too pretty a name for me, and I didn't deserve it. Maybe it was a cruel joke or another chance to not be attached to an identity. I was also learning that feeling unlovable and not good enough was a core belief of the entire human race.

"I love it," I said, waiting for the bad news to hit. But there was no bad news. He walked off and went back inside. I just stood there motionless, breathing in what had happened in the blink of an eye. What's amazing is that I didn't have to ask people to call me Giselle once the word got around in the Buddha Field. They just did. The outside world was another story. Some people had a really hard time with me changing my name. It was a good exercise in not caring what others thought, as I'm sure I got a lot of snickers and rolling of the eyes as people heard about my name change. To me, it was a beautiful gift, and I appreciate it to this day. But then again, being made to feel "special" was an elixir for me.

As the months flew by, I really wanted to move inside The Master's house to do service.

There was no denying that there was some sort of energetic transmission in the company of The Master. It was something I had never heard about before, but I knew I experienced it. It was like a blissful force field around him. Some would just call it shakti.

One day, I was reading a gorgeous book called *The Bliss of Freedom* by Master Charles. He describes this transmission as "the process of entrainment, wherein, according to the principles of sound, the lower frequency sound can pull others toward its slower vibration and greater amplitude, so the energy field of the enlightening master entrains or empowers that of the student, until ultimately the experience of an enlightening state of being, an unending awareness of God, or Source, becomes constant." *Wow, am I in the right place or what?* I thought. This was very seductive to me and firmly planted the desire to be around The Master as much as possible. I had to fight the ambitious me who wanted to create a strategy, and just make it happen. But I wanted to be one of those special people close to him.

The Master addressed this ambition to be special with me once while I was in the chair. He shared with me that the qualities of being clever and calculating were not something that ever helped you go to God. In the Bhagavad Gita, Krishna tells Arjuna that it is through innocence that you go to God.

"Go find Giselle, quick!" I heard Lucy yell from the side door of The Master's house. I was in the front yard cleaning out flowerbeds and was glad to get up and out of the hot Texas sun.

"He wants to see you," she said as she rushed me into the side door of the house, like a secret service agent. I stepped in and looked around. I was standing in what was formerly the garage but was now a fitness room. I saw Pilates equipment, an elliptical trainer, and a ballet bar against the wall. The Master was running on the elliptical machine, and I was to stand directly in front of him so he would not have to turn his head.

"Thank you for inviting me inside," I said. "In fact, I've wanted to come inside for a long time."

"So why have you stayed out?" he asked. I honestly did not know why I felt like I could never enter the house. I suddenly had a moment where I realized I had been my own prison guard, keeping myself away from what I truly wanted. I wondered where else in my life I was denying what I truly wanted.

The next several days seemed to be an unfolding of the same message. How much did I keep myself from my true heart's desire of reaching enlightenment and why? Who had made these rules? I held myself hostage to so many things like what people thought, what I could do in life, how to behave, what I should want, what my ceiling of success was, and more. I was basically a prisoner of my own mind. I saw how I had put so many limits on myself. I had been seeing myself only as others saw me instead of being unlimited in anything I wanted to achieve in my career or in my personal definition of happiness and contentment. I had put a cap on all my dreams, telling myself they were out of my reach. I was controlled by all the constructs, walls, and limitations I had accumulated and didn't even know I had. Later that day, I wrote:

DESIGN JOB

The furniture has been rearranged
I've seen the dirt under the sofa
The upholstery has been ripped off
Leaving a frame
That the ego still wants to recover
The room is looking pretty empty
Wait
Now the walls are coming down
Oh my
And the ceiling just got blown off
I am now thanking God for the floor under my feet
Until it disintegrates
Now there is just space
What is left to hold on to?
Just the idea there is space
Please take even the idea

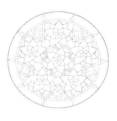

CHAPTER 20

Behind Closed Doors

From then on, I seemed to be part of daily life inside the house, which was our ashram. It was a typical 1970s' style single-story, tan brick ranch home, in a very suburban neighborhood in south Austin. The front yard was well manicured, with many attendants constantly doing yard service. There were trees, roses, and other flowers with a large mowed yard.

Upon entering the house, one stepped into a small hallway which led to the living room, with several doors leading to the bedrooms. The lighting was very dim, and there was an enormous array of statues sitting around: Buddhas, Buddha heads, Quan yin, Krishna, and even one of Ramakrishna. There was a sofa and several comfortable chairs. By day, this room served as a meditation/waiting room for those waiting to see The Master for cleansing.

I floated between outside service and inside service, always preferring inside. That is where all the action was. The Master lived there, along with four or five roommates/attendants, and there was plenty going on. Service, cooking, cleaning, cleansing, personality clashes, lots of meditating, and the daily protocol of The Master's schedule. It took a small army to fulfill all the duties. He always told us that he didn't really need anyone to do anything for him, but we needed to do it for us. I actually believed this at the time.

It must be amazing to live here, I thought at the time. I sometimes helped in the kitchen, which was challenging because the closer you got to him, the more intense the service would become. The kitchen was territory fiercely protected by the hens in charge. There were always several people preparing his meals, cleaning, or sometimes just organizing Tupperware! On certain days, the kitchen was run by a woman with a very strong personality, and she expected you to be one-pointed with your service, at all times. She was a tough boss, and a workhorse herself but definitely could have her sweet moments.

The Master occasionally passed through the kitchen, and everyone would stop to have open-eye meditation with him. Sometimes he offered guidance to someone or shared something from a letter he was reading. He received handfuls of letters from devotees every week.

After lunch, he would "see" people for cleansing. Not everyone got to see *him* for cleansing, as many people just saw Jeff at another location. It could take years for the privilege of seeing The Master for cleansing, if ever.

"LOVE ME, LOVE ME, LOVE ME!" I screamed and cried at the top of my lungs. These words were often the final part of my cleansing sessions with him. The screams were usually related to my wounded father relationship, the death of my sister, the suicide of my boyfriend, and the emotional neglect I suffered through.

When I worked with Jeff, things tended to focus on the psychological level. We were always trying to get to the root of a problem. Not feeling good enough, not feeling lovable, and not feeling like I deserved love were common themes with me, based on my imprinting. Slowly, we began to peel the layers of the onion. After a point, I began to recognize when the ego was taking over. I was then able to have a more detached view of the situation and see it is as "Oh, that again." When I complained about something like not being included, not feeling acknowledged, or if the comparing mind took over, Maximus would often say, "How old are you right now?" That tended to stop me in my tracks. Of course he learned that from The Master, and it is a brilliant but annoying question to ask anyone in the middle of a drama.

Cleansing with The Master went deeper in that he had incredible insights and vision into your life. He said he could see past karmas and past lives, and he would occasionally give you shakti after you were finished. The sessions were emotionally rough, however. Things buried inside would get stirred, and often I felt a lot worse after leaving. Sometimes I felt the burden of lifetimes leave, and I would feel like a new baby. But it was never a walk in the park.

The cleansing took place in his bedroom. He sat in his red chair, one of the only two chairs he ever used. The chair was an actual airplane seat that formed to his body, and it traveled with him like a movable throne. His other chair was a portable version that was carried more often. Whoever positioned the chair carried a level to make sure the chair was perfectly level with the ground at all times.

"So how is the dream of Giselle?" he began as I took my seat in the black leather Eames chair that was placed directly in front of him. His gaze always arrested me in a way that threw me in to the present moment. He was completely present, like no one I had ever met.

I would begin to tell him what was happening in my life, and the session would take off from there. Many times I would bring up feeling neglected by my boyfriend Maximus, fighting with my ex-husband over raising the children, and other dramas. There was always a box of tissues because once you sat in front of The Master, inevitably there were tears. Many people, including myself, used a nearby pillow for hitting and releasing anger. There was no limit as to how loud you were permitted to scream. Usually, like that day, I let it out. I later learned that you could tell who was receiving cleansing by the hoarseness in the recipient's voice the next day.

Quite often during the session, you could ask for guidance. And advice was available. Guidance was considered a gift, and not everyone received it. It seems that those that followed the guidance most often tended to receive it more and more. Following guidance was a major part of discipleship, because it was surrendering to The Master. The purpose was to help you stay focused on the highest, and not get distracted by whatever else was happening. Also, he wanted to help you avoid karmas of which you were unaware. Receiving guidance was ultimately designed to help you avoid samsaras, which are the uncooked seeds of desire that could easily sprout and "take you on a trip" or into a place in your mind full of questions and doubt. If you were unable to avoid these karmic patterns, you were doomed to repeat the same suffering for many more lifetimes.

This karmic reality was illustrated in the story of the disciple who went to get The Master a drink of water and ran into someone along the way. This distraction made him forget his original task—bringing water to The Master. This excursion led to more and more distractions until ten years had passed. Eventually, the man returns with the water and delivers it to The Master. The teaching was that it is very easy to get distracted and then to "miss" an important lifetime.

The guidance disciples received was never what the ego wanted, especially if it involved wanting to travel. The Master rarely advised anyone to travel. On one occasion, I was invited to go to Egypt with a friend, and I was eager to go. I had always dreamed of visiting the pyramids and immersing myself in the exotic and ancient culture I had only heard of since I was a girl. After asking if I should book the trip, his reply was simple:

"There is no *there* there. There is only *hereness*, so why go?" he said. I didn't go.

I once asked if it would be a good idea to take up Golden Shield Qi Gong. My girlfriend in the Buddha Field, Jaquetta, had taken up the practice—a powerful and beautiful martial art focused on longevity and health, created five hundred years ago in western China. I was attracted to the skills that centered and empowered one's energy.

But The Master did not agree. "Do not practice Golden Shield. It is empowering and not what is needed for you. I want to take you to a place beyond enemies, from the place of needing to protect yourself to the place where there is no enemy."

I also asked about personal financial deals. I was curious about whether or not to invest in an oil deal that business associates had brought to me.

"There is oil. Whether or not you find it depends on greed and what is to be done with the money. It depends on whether or not it serves the light. What happens when a child bites a mother's teat? She is not happy. That is what taking the oil is like to Mother Earth."

Another burning question was about what my true dharma was. Dharma is about one's life purpose, what you are supposed to be doing with your life. I always felt like I had so many roles to play and was spread too thin. First, I was a now a single mother. Second, I was a yoga instructor who was teaching more and more. Third, I was an entrepreneur who invested in real estate projects. Then, of course, I was a devotee who made myself available for service several days a week in the garden, and at least three or four nights a week with the group. I admired those who had just one thing on their plate, not three or four. I was almost afraid to ask what my true dharma was, because I feared it would be something like bookkeeping. But when I was considering teaching more yoga classes, I just had to ask.

The Master told me in a matter-of-fact way that my dharma was simple. "Your dharma is to serve me directly." An excitement rose in me, because this had been my heart's desire. This was an official invitation to be in his inner circle. I would have the chance to be physically near him much more often now. I resisted asking all the questions like when, where, and how, and I decided to simply follow his guidance: "Be in love with the not knowing."

He went on to explain my discipleship. "What I see with this personality [me] is a period of great insightfulness and then allurement back into the world." Often, when my questions were about mundane decisions, he would tell me that my indecision would go away with more meditation. I recommitted to my meditation practice.

When I was having a problem letting go of a relationship, The Master said, "What is love never changes. What is not love, always changes." At the time, this was profound for me. Many times I was insecure in my relationship with Maximus, either feeling neglected or in fear of losing it. I was challenged to focus on love as a force that is always there and not something that comes and goes. I began to understand that it was my perception and fears that come and go. Even if I did lose my boyfriend, there would still be love, just transmuted into a different form.

When I was really hard on myself about something like being jealous or envious, The Master offered this: "See a personality trait as just that. Do not condemn yourself for it." Whenever I did feel jealous toward someone or competitive with other females, I would judge myself harshly. The reality was that my programming was to compete with other women (my sisters) for the attention of the male (my father). Then I would feel self-hatred for feeling jealous and competitive.

I surrendered to The Master's guidance because he would continually say, "Through total surrender comes total freedom." While many of his teachings were sage, this one seemed deadly. I would later interpret it to mean "Through total surrender of oneself to The Master comes total confusion." Or "When you give up yourself, your instincts, or your power completely to another, you lose yourself." However, it would be years before I would believe this.

One of my mentors at the time was The Master's driver and confidant, Barry. I envied his close proximity to The Master and consistently made myself available to him. We both brought similar skills to the table, including worldly experience in business and professional relationships. I remember at one point I was washing and folding Barry's clothes. He was great at getting people to do things. In fact, I didn't even fold my own clothes. Mariela took care of that at home. Barry was very intelligent, a good creator and an expert in manifesting. We were both entrepreneurial, and he often bounced ideas off me.

"I have a really important idea I want to talk to you about, Giselle," he said one day. "It has to do with a very high service for The Master." He had my complete attention. *Anything for The Master*, I thought.

"It has two aspects," he explained. "First, The Master never lets anyone do a service involving money. He just doesn't allow it. And second, you could help out a situation that needs to go away."

I was beginning to feel really important, and I was intrigued.

"But what about Maximus? He's really good with money, and I know he helps people buy houses and sometimes buys them himself and rents them to devotees. He handles money," I responded.

"Yes, but The Master doesn't want Maximus to know about this for other reasons. It's important that he absolutely not know about this," said Barry. This really appealed to my sense of importance and the idea of having a higher service than Maximus. It wasn't lost on me that even through all of my transcendent experiences, I still wanted to feel important.

"OK, so here's what it is. We want to buy out the person who bought this house for The Master. The woman who bought it wants out, and we want to buy it from her. She is asking only for enough money to pay off the loan, and she already has put quite a lot of money into it. The Master said it would be alright if you bought it. But you cannot tell anyone and we have to be really careful about whose name we put it in. We, of course, don't ever want anyone to find out he lives here. It cannot be in his name."

I would have to think about this. It was a lot of money. Six figures. Well, what better charitable contribution could I make than supporting the one who was bringing so much consciousness to the world, the one who was living his whole life to help us wake up? Besides, total surrender equals total freedom. I decided I would have to do it. I wanted total freedom—total enlightenment.

I bought the house with the money from my divorce settlement. No one in my family knew about it, and no one would ever find out. The closing consisted of me, Barry, the closing agent, and a large pile of cash. But before the closing happened, we spent weeks creating a blind trust so that no one's name would be tied to the property, thus protecting everyone's identity. It took a while to figure out how to do this and also have a provision so that the beneficiary of the trust could be changed by The Master at any time, to whomever he wanted.

It was a complicated legal document, and this would not be the last time I would deal with it.

These were the golden years of discipleship. I loved my life. I knew where I was going: enlightenment. It had been my dream since I was eleven. I felt fortunate to have found an awakened master in this lifetime. I had been given a map and a new way to live by someone I believed was already there. I was experiencing periods of peace. And when I wasn't, I usually knew how to detach enough to become the witness to my own human drama. My real spiritual growth was in that I knew the real battle was with the mind and the ego's desire to always be in control. I was learning how to be present, and I knew my education was not about perfecting the ego, but going beyond the ego. I was also privy to the sacred teachings of The Master, including sacred breathing that I could use on a moment-to-moment basis. There was a breath technique to use all day that brought peace, known as the shakti breath. There was a strong and powerful breathing technique I used while sitting, called the ascending breath. And then, of course, there was the formal practice of sitting and being magnetized by God, which I practiced every morning and every evening for about an hour at a time. Meditation was at the core of my new existence.

The ultimate experience we were all waiting for was the direct experience of God. This was my true heart's desire. I didn't really know in what form it would come, but it was something The Master revealed when it was time. It was known as "The Knowing." I had read in Osho's *Book of Secrets*, from the teachings of Atisha, that there is a place in your spiritual development where you need a master to take you on the final part of your journey. To me this is what "The Knowing" represented: the final aspect that one couldn't achieve alone.

By no means were these simple little techniques. They were transformative energetic teachings revealed by The Master at various stages of our awakening. They opened channels in the body, and then we practiced them every day for years. When you were really focusing, you were practicing every single moment and with every single breath. Meditation was the way, and I fell in love with it. It was like taking a seat on a royal throne. Everything falls away except what is real.

I had favorite places to meditate when I was not home. I thought nothing about finding a big shade tree anywhere in the city and just pulling my car over. I would turn off the engine, open the window, and close my eyes. Blissful. If it was sunset,

I had a favorite spot in the back parking lot of Barton Springs pool. I would put the tailgate down on my truck, lay out a yoga blanket, and meditate, sometimes with my eyes open, sometimes closed.

Once I had one of the most powerfully transformative experiences of my life. It was dusk, and I had my eyes closed. As I opened them, I melted into the scene I was witnessing. Or maybe the scene melted into me. There was no difference. It was all one big luminous soup. A man with his little girl, the tree under which they were standing, the light, me—we were all one ecstatic vibration that beautifully and peacefully merged. I was complete within myself and wouldn't have minded dying at that moment. It felt as though I would never need anything ever again. Eventually I had the thought that I never ever wanted to leave this state of being. And as I had this thought, reality became denser and I contracted, becoming a separate thing once again.

Knowing that this reality exists at all times is a saving grace for me. Even if I cannot reproduce this experience at will, one taste of it was enough to keep me practicing forever. When I had a chance to share this with someone, I was reminded that waking up was not just about peak experiences, but the moment-to-moment choice of the highest. It's not what happens sometimes, it's what happens all the time, in every moment.

GRATITUDE

Sometimes I look for the gratitude
Sometimes I swell with gratitude
And sometimes I ejaculate gratitude
Through my eyes
It just explodes

CHAPTER 21

The Flowering

If this book were a movie, this chapter would be a film montage of happy blissful scenes with flowers and smiles and sunshine and kisses and blankets in the park and long hair and many "wow" discoveries—my own private 60s revolution. But the revolution was within: white hot and quiet.

In this flower power era, my expression of this love was in full bloom. I filled notebooks with drawings and poems and insights about this love I was experiencing. I was still obsessed with making flower mandalas. It was my regular offering made to the divine with love and devotion.

One day at a group gathering, it was announced that there would be a large celebration. There would be a dance party with a full-on ballroom production. I was so excited. I had the idea to make a huge mandala out of roses as a vertical backdrop for The Master while he shared satsang.

So we did. James built an almost eight-foot by eight-foot upright wooden square with chicken wire on the face. We ordered two thousand roses, in every single color under the sun. Nearly one quarter of the ballroom was filled with buckets of roses. The perfume floated in the air. We organized them by color so that there would be a gradation of color covering the whole rainbow spectrum. Starting in the middle, I placed each fully opened fresh dewy flower in a pattern of concentric circles, continuing one rose at a time, until the eight foot square was completely covered. It was an orgy of exploding color, delicate texture, and the intoxicating scent of roses. This set the tone for a party of sharing and dancing that went early into the morning, as usual.

There was special joy in that mandala as I had brought my children along to help during the day. I had begun to bring them whenever I could for simple services and felt gratified to include them. They were getting to know my friends and even forming some friendships with the few other Buddha Field kids.

Shortly after that joyous celebration, I got a call from someone designated to inform me about any Buddha Field activity.

"It's just too risky. We cannot go there for a while." Apparently, we had to stop going to the Global Theater for classes because we were "being watched." We didn't know who was watching us, or at least it was not information they wanted to share with me. But as usual, things got around, and I found out that there was a bigger story. Someone had written an e-mail that went out to a group in the community, and it was potentially very damaging. The story told to me was that this was from someone's boyfriend who had not been invited into the group and was not happy about it. Also, he was upset that his girlfriend was taking advice from the so-called leader and he felt she was being controlled by him. As a result, this caused huge problems in their relationship. The e-mail went on to accuse the group of being a cult. It further went on to accuse The Master of being a fraud, a criminal, and a fugitive. The author was going to expose the whole group for "what it was." Even though this was not the first time such accusations had been made, it still brought up some fear for me because this was the first time a threat to the group had transpired since my involvement. After 9/11 and the war on terrorism, cults were seen as a national threat.

We all became even more conscious of protecting what we had. The general public would never understand. And worse, people would easily misunderstand what we were doing. The consequence of the wrong kind of exposure was incredibly scary. But even in my devotion and fear of losing my beloved group, I still allowed myself to consider, if only for a few moments, that this was a cult. But I quickly dismissed my doubts. We were simply not for the masses, and that was all. How could the general public be expected to understand? The world was a place filled with fear, conditioning, and judgment. I wanted to be as far away from that as possible. I had found solace from the mass mind-set, and I didn't want to let it go.

I was troubled by the turn of events and became concerned enough to call a lawyer for advice. I called on behalf of the Buddha Field to see if there was anything we could do to prevent this kind of slander. The information I got was that a slander case was very hard to prove, and it probably would just go away. Plus, taking it to court would make everything even more public. We were advised that we could proceed with a restraining order, but since we couldn't confirm who had written the e-mail, it would be pointless. As far as the public went, who would ever believe such a story? It was decided to let the controversy die down. But I took the legal counsel's advice to The Master because I felt strongly that something should be done to prevent this from happening again.

We relocated to an exercise studio at the south end of town. It was not nearly as nice as the theater, and was a lot smaller. The lighting was not good either. We had been spoiled with plush comfortable seats, theater lighting, and plenty of room. After all, our classes could last from five to seven hours in one sitting. And there was only one bathroom, which was challenging for one hundred and twenty people who were sitting for so long. But we adjusted. It was more important that we all stayed together.

One of the highlights of class in this new space was the night David did a striptease. David was an exceptional-looking young man who had an irresistible combination of masculinity, grace, intelligence, and humility. He was tall with short, closely cropped hair, deep-set eyes, and a body to rival Michelangelo's statue of David. I don't think there was anyone who didn't either admire him or want to sleep with him.

One typical class night, The Master said, "David, do a strip-tease."

Since the ability to "drop your mind" and "be a yes" were some of the qualities that The Master was cultivating in us, David immediately stood up. The crowd roared with catcalls and encouragement, as *everyone* wanted to see this.

The Master then put his hand in the air to pause all activity, like Caesar hushing the crowd. He turned to Cliff, the house DJ.

"Cliff, put on something appropriate," he directed. After a few moments, a perfect striptease song came on over the speakers.

At this point all eyes were on David. He blushed, took a breath, slowly stood up, and began to move. It was impossible for him not to be graceful. He slithered and slowly gyrated to the music and began to remove one piece of clothing after another, slinging and swinging each article into the group. He had never done this before, but he was amazing.

The group participated as well. Maximus, who had some real experience in this line of work, walked up to him and put a dollar bill in his tiny briefs. Others followed by throwing money, screaming with delight and excitement. The crowd roared. David stopped at his barely-there briefs and finished dancing until the end of the music, on cue. It was a fantastically fun and arousing performance—not all that unusual for class.

On another occasion, Orbis stripped down and streaked across the floor of the theater completely naked. He wasn't instructed to do this, but he volunteered. We all performed elaborate skits with great fanfare every Halloween, and Orbis usually played a porn star.

People spent weeks producing skits, writing scripts, finding directors, and making costumes that were wickedly fun. We often parodied TV shows and movies such as *Six Feet Under* and *Lord of the Rings*. Some people played saints and mystics in very moving performances. There was even one with current political figures, including Hillary Clinton and George Bush in drag. Many times, people used these skits as an excuse to dress in drag, play a prostitute, or express a part of their shadow selves they could never otherwise show.

I was also in a skit based on the TV show *The L Word*. I played a wealthy, brunette, English lesbian. In one scene, I "go down" on my girlfriend. We were fully dressed and performing the scene melodramatically. With added flourish, I even ended the skit by wiping my mouth after the dramatic sexual escapade. Anything went.

All of this was magnificent training that taught us how to let go of our egos and what other people thought of us. It was impossible to participate in exercises like these without being totally vulnerable and present to the moment.

CHAPTER 22

The Knowing

It was during this period at our new space that I became more aware of the politics of the group. Even though we liked to think of ourselves as beyond politics, there were definitely little factions. It was often said that there was no hierarchy, and maybe there wasn't in The Master's eyes. But the disciples knew that it existed.

The hierarchy was structured between two main groups: those who had "the knowing" and those who didn't. The "knowing" was ultimately what we were all there for, so it was quite a distinction. I perceived those that had the knowing to be more evolved, wiser, and closer to enlightenment. If you weren't "clear" about something or if you were struggling, someone with the "knowing" was your go-to person. They were imbued with "knowing" more and therefore could see clearly where you were getting stuck. And here's a hint: it was always the mind or the ego.

There were eight or ten people who had received the "knowing" years before. In fact, there had not been a "knowing session" for at least twelve years. Of course, there was a lot of speculation as to why that was. All I knew at the time was that I wanted to have the direct experience of God.

It was also during this period that we were fully living the life of disciples as directed by The Master. It is one thing to read about sacred teachings. But it is an entirely different matter to have the opportunity to become totally immersed in the teachings and act on them in the modern world. We were modern-day yogis. We did not have to go to India, live in an ashram, or isolate ourselves in a cave in the Himalayas. We could do it right in the middle of twenty-first century America, under everyone's noses and without anyone knowing. This life was total immersion. We all suspended the "shoulds" of the way the rest of the world was living, and dove deeply into devotional life. This was a mystery school after all—an alchemical process where base metal turned to gold.

THE MOUNTAIN TOP

I lie willingly on the table like a wounded sparrow
Fragile and bland
As you carve away with laser precision
Transforming me into a bird, exotic and never-before-seen
And as I think I am ready to take flight
I realize I never was a bird
Through your deep, tender, delicate and artistic mastery,
You are showing me this life as it is
I am on the mountaintop with you seeing Reality

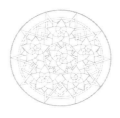

CHAPTER 23

The Lifestyle

"Hey, get me some extra pickles!" I yelled out of the car window at my friend Jaquetta. She was my Buddha Field girlfriend and confidante. She was also a fellow yoga teacher, which seemed particularly amusing when we stopped to get barbecue and Diet Cokes. We didn't have a problem being ourselves. We were not trying to be above other people in any aspect of our Buddha Field presence. We shared our lives and our stories and just had fun together. We talked about boys. And girls. We were that one phone call we could always make when we were going crazy about something. We always told each other that we had each other's back. We liked each other immediately when we met at my first gathering. She was the one who had given the Quan Yin statue, and I treasured it.

We stopped for a quick bite to eat on our way to satsang after seeing a ballet performance with the Buddha Field at the Global Theater. Our schedules were at breakneck speed, so we had to make it quick. We were immersed in the mystery school twenty-four hours a day. The actual time we spent together was phenomenal, and our schedules were intense.

Monday night was satsang. We divided up into small groups and went to someone's home for an evening of satsang as shared by someone in "the knowing," followed by meditation. These were intimate gatherings where everyone had a chance to share personal experiences, and we all usually did. Tuesday night was a night off, but a lot of the time we were doing service of some kind. Wednesday night was ballet class for those who were invited to attend. Thursday night was class, which took anywhere from four to six hours, sometimes seven. Friday night was an occasional outing or at least a late-afternoon swim at Barton Springs for a select few. Saturday night was off. Sunday night was usually a movie followed by a celebration. There were also very elaborate parties at Christmas and Thanksgiving. And, of course, there was the occasional Sunday afternoon outing. This schedule did not include your daily service. For me, I was working in the garden twice a week while the kids were in school. This left Tuesday, Wednesday, Friday, and Saturday evenings with the kids. I no longer had a social life outside the Buddha Field, which was part of The Master's master plan. And if my boyfriend hadn't been a member, I would never have seen him; also part of The Master's plan.

The scheduling, although intense, became easier to deal with because the schedule was fairly consistent. I found a young woman who was coming in to the Buddha Field, but had not yet been invited to meet The Master. Therefore, she was free and happy to babysit in the evenings during the weeks when the kids were with me. The kids loved her, and it was nice to have someone who knew what I was up to and could understand my sometimes being three hours late. Because there was a set schedule, the children came to accept that on Mondays I was teaching yoga and on Thursdays, I was at class.

Christmas day was a very special celebration that started at about one in the afternoon and went far into the evening at the theater, with gifts exchanged and hours of shakti given. I did not consider the Buddha Field Christian; it was spiritual but not religious. The Master often spoke about how Christianity was the misunderstanding of Christ, and Buddhism was the misunderstanding of Buddha. In other words, those teachers had truth to share. But the organizations built around those teachings didn't always carry the pure message of the teacher. On Christmas day The Master would speak beautifully about the Christ consciousness that was in every human being and how the awakening of that consciousness was every human being's divine journey.

However, planning to be away from my family on Christmas afternoon was a nightmare. I get a stomachache just writing this because of the stress this always caused me. The planning with my family was meticulous in order for this to happen and for no one to feel slighted. Basically a schedule was established every year. I had the children on Christmas Eve and until noon on Christmas day. It was really hard to pack up the little ones in their pajamas and say good-bye.

Besides the time and space aspects of the disciple's life, there was the code of living, which included an adoption of behaviors, morals, diet, and language. This way of life mirrored a view of the world according to The Master.

I remember at one point I began to feel like being in a relationship with Maximus was forbidden. I thought I would be guided not to see him. This was very early when I naively thought that a devoutly spiritual path required the renouncement of all worldly possessions and needs—including intimate relationships. I thought I would have to give up any attachments I had, but I certainly did not want to give up this relationship. I was relieved to learn that it was the attachment to things we were to give up, not necessarily the things themselves. For example, I could enjoy a relationship with my boyfriend. But if I got to the point where I had to have the relationship to feel whole or be happy, then that was an attachment. I told myself that it was okay to be in a romantic relationship because I wasn't attached to my relationship. Well, that was a lie. I was also attached to my children, relationships I would never give up. Never.

But with Maximus, I was attached because of our deep friendship, which still exists today. We shared devotion to truth, which reinforced an even deeper bond between us. But eventually our romantic relationship came to an end. It seemed that the rigid structure of our eating, our schedules, and our following every ounce of guidance took the juice out of the relationship. It dried up. Also, Maximus never really took responsibility for any action that contributed to the demise of our relationship. I finally realized I no longer needed someone to play the teacher role at every moment. I was being taught by The Master. I began to resent Maximus, and resentment was a road I did not want to take. Eventually, we started spending less and less time with each other, until one day I realized that the only thing we were still doing together was swimming. And even that was no longer personal. He began to invite his young female roommate to join us. She was becoming his new project of physical transformation, a fact that hurt my feelings regardless of our pulling apart. However, it is still hard for me to have anything but grateful feelings for Maximus and all that we were to each other. Our time together had come to an end.

No longer in a relationship, I was missing physical intimacy. I asked The Master about this the first chance I got.

"I really want some clarity on still feeling so attached to the desires of the body. I am struggling with a strong sex drive,"

I told him during a private cleansing session. I was confused about sexuality and spirituality. "Is it spiritual to have a sex life?" I asked.

He answered, "What is sex? It is just an energy. It is shakti. Let it rise. Instead of sexual frustration, feel the shakti, rising and ecstatic. Sex is an idea. When sexual energy occurs, know that it is shakti. At this point in your evolution, Giselle, to go for sexual experiences is to go for the bondage, the attachment, the suffering. Just be in the ecstatic energy and let it flow through the body. How can you soar in the heavens if you are still earthbound and attached to anything here?"

I was a well-meaning devotee, but this was a little too advanced for me. I just couldn't imagine celibacy. This part of my spiritual journey was confusing. All around the Buddha Field I saw the spectrum of sexuality, from promiscuity to celibacy. I was neither of these. I liked being in a committed relationship, exploring intimacy and depth with one partner. And what about The Master? Little did I know that he had a very active sex life—with devotees.

CHAPTER 24

Satsang at My House

"If you could meet a modern-day Yogananda right now, would you drop everything and go?" Emily posed the question to the tall and dashing Jim Morrison look-alike at Whole Foods. She was a devotee, grabbing a bite to eat before a large celebration at my house. The man she was talking with had just gotten off a plane from Switzerland and was meeting his parents for a bite to eat when he noticed Emily. She was an attractive, brunette, tan woman staring at him. I'm sure he was used to this, because he definitely drew a lot of attention himself. He was extremely handsome.

"Uh yeah, sure," he said. He looked and sounded a bit jet-lagged. She looked deeply into his eyes and held her gaze, which seemed to mesmerize this handsome stranger. "I mean right now," she said. "Like, we go now." She grabbed his hand and led him toward the door. They were then on their way to my house. He would be my next relationship, and Emily was literally delivering him to my front door.

Hosting a satsang at my house was an effortless production and a privilege I really enjoyed. My living room could easily hold one hundred and fifty people. In my upper-class neighborhood, at least sixty or more cars would all drive up like locusts on the prairie. Then there would be a parade of people carrying folding chairs, pillows, and Tupperware from the bottom of the hill. Fortunately, it was one of those neighborhoods where large-scale fundraisers were quite common and, amazing as it sounds, no one ever complained.

But one day I ran into two neighborhood women in the grocery store. They wanted to know why I had not invited them to whatever it was I was having with "all those gorgeous men!" I replied, "Well it's a yoga teacher meeting. Sorry." I had been instructed to say that it was a movie group, but found that excuse too lame for my discriminating neighbors. They believed it.

They were accurate about the gorgeous men. Of course there were gorgeous women, too. In fact, on several nights, I got my video camera and stood on the front porch and just videotaped everyone strolling in for an evening of celebration with The Master. I wondered why so many of the devotees handpicked by The Master were physically attractive. I had always wondered about this. What does physical appearance have to do with spirituality? I even videotaped The Master, which was forbidden, driving up in his "Popemobile." His driver would always go very slow, "pope speed," for maximum "pope viewing." The arrival of the Buddha Field was quite a procession.

Once inside, the procession continued. Upstairs one hundred and twenty people sat very still in meditation on pillows and chairs. I took great pleasure in selecting the music that played. The Master's chair was brought in and readied, surrounded by large vases of roses and candles. Someone laid out a long piece of silk fabric for him to walk through the crowd on in order to reach his seat. Downstairs, The Master was in the guest room with various members of his entourage, waiting to make his entrance. I waited for him at the bottom of the stairwell, to walk him up.

As he walked out of the guest room and came toward me, I felt like this was a very high moment. Not just because of the celebration energy, but I had the feeling that we were at the peak of something, right then, in that moment. As we looked into each other's eyes, we were two people in the prime of life, doing what they loved, serving what they loved, radiating health, love, God, and experiencing the highest in the physical world. It was all coming together in a moment frozen in my mind forever.

"I am going to slap you," he said softly after a very long gaze, even with so many people waiting upstairs.

My mind came barreling back into focus as I wondered, "What is he talking about?"

"With shakti," he said. He grazed his hand gently over my face without touching it, never losing eye contact. Then he did it again. I closed my eyes as I was swept into another vibration that flooded my heart center with a warm liquid, the divine nectar. With that, he continued to walk upstairs, took his seat, and began the evening. I soon followed and sat on my cushion near him. He talked about the movie we had seen earlier, and then we got out the guitars for hours of singing. The acoustics in the room were very conducive to a large choir such as this. The ceiling was domed with the highest part at least eighteen feet tall. We were all in a cathedral of sound. He directed us like a choral master, all of our vocal instruments vibrating in perfect unison. The energy kept getting higher and higher. For me, it was a glorious celebration of indescribable joy. The entire house was vibrating with ecstatic energy.

At some point I turned around to look at the room. I froze as I noticed someone I had never seen before. This was very unusual because no one got invited out of the blue; that could take years. I noticed that as I looked at him, he was looking directly at me. Then we had THE LOOK. I turned back around. The look and the energy exchanged between us swirled around this otherworldly evening. After hours and hours of laughing, singing, sharing, and being enchanted by The Master, everyone vaporized en masse just as they had appeared. A few stayed to help me move the furniture and return the room to its normal arrangement. It was a glorious night.

I realized that I could have experienced that same evening in so many different ways. It could have been a nice evening of song and merriment—a fun time singing and joking with friends. It could have been an average evening consumed by whatever the ego was obsessing about. But instead, it was truly transcendent. It was almost as if I had a choice in how I could experience life, at every moment. I felt like I was beginning to understand the phrase "heaven on earth." As The Master said, "You don't go to heaven. Heaven comes to you. Heaven is a state of being."

Later in the evening, well after midnight, I was sitting at my kitchen table talking on the phone and savoring every aspect of the evening. *How could life get any better than this*, I thought?

Just then, I heard a knock on the door. A chill ran down my spine. It was very late by this time, and the sudden noise scared me. I was home alone in this big house, sitting in the kitchen, surrounded by glass. Anyone could see me, although I couldn't see them. I got off the phone and without walking up to the door, I yelled, "Who is it?"

"Are you up?" I didn't recognize the male voice. I hesitated before walking to the front door. When I got a glimpse of the stranger, I recognized him from the gathering. He said that he had left something upstairs and asked if he could retrieve it.

"Of course," I said.

As he left, I walked outside with him and saw a big black 1956 Cadillac in the driveway. Being a classic car enthusiast, I immediately walked up to the open window and peeked in. Inside, sprawled across the backseat, was the stranger with whom I had shared THE LOOK at the gathering earlier. I was surprised and excited to see him.

"Let's go for a ride," I blurted out without thinking. And that we did. That night it was just a ride in the car, but I knew that there was a bigger ride in store for the two of us. His name was Joaquin, and we talked for what seemed like hours. The other stranger was his seventeen-year-old son. It was just the three of us. It was so natural and easy, like we had been friends for years. We planned a future road trip, complete with a shopping list of items needed: Ray Ban sunglasses, road map, thermos of coffee, and a box of glazed Dunkin' Donuts.

Strangely, I didn't see him for quite a while. He was still involved in a relationship, and I had just gotten out of one. I knew he traveled abroad most of the time, and I didn't really expect to see him. There were a few times that I saw him in the garden or at various satsangs, but we rarely spoke. Life went on.

Over the years, I was spending more time at The Master's house, doing service directly for him. What I had really wanted to happen was happening. Because of my close proximity, I began to know about his personal life. I learned that his first name was Andreas, and those closest to him addressed him with this name. I learned that he wore make-up, a little eyeliner and some mascara or false lashes. I was sent to Saks one day to buy his favorite eyeliner and concealer. I also found out he loved to watch beauty pageants like *Miss Universe*. I learned that he was gay, and he had a boyfriend.

When I first learned that he was in a sexual relationship, I was surprised. I somehow had the idea, as do a lot of people, that if you are enlightened, you are beyond the desires of the body. Isn't this what he had expressed to me, raising the sexual energy to spiritual energy? But the truth was that I didn't have enlightened friends to whom I could compare him. After I had digested this fact, it made perfect sense to me. Enlightenment was not a state where you were free *from* living this human experience, but free *to* fully live this human experience. Or, as I had heard it later from Isha, another teacher, to be fully divine you must be fully human. It was all making sense to me.

There were many moments in my life in which I really felt free—free from judgment, free from the fear of what other people thought, free to be friends with whomever I wanted, free to be intimate with whomever I wanted, free to dress in ways that expressed who I was, free to live my life as I wanted and free from "shoulds." I felt free to not feel obligated to what others expected from me about how to live my life, and I felt free to pursue my heart's desire. My whole life was a movement toward freedom, and it was becoming my reality. I wasn't becoming free from sexual desire, but when the desire happened I was free to fully enjoy it. So how could I hold any judgment against Andreas? I couldn't.

CHAPTER 25

The Empire Crumbles

Class had moved location once again. We were now in the center of town, near Barton Springs, in an old lodge. It was strange to be meeting right in the heart of Austin, near the Springs. It didn't feel very discreet at all.

This magnificent group had gone through a metamorphosis over the years. For some reason, the move to this space marked a change in everyone. I noticed how certain individuals had become very jaded. It happened to everyone from time to time, including me. This seemed to take place in time with the rhythmic contraction and expansion that naturally happens in the evolution of consciousness. On any given day you would just not be into "it." Maybe you weren't feeling as fresh. Maybe you thought the class exercises were boring. Maybe you just hated everyone in the group. Maybe you thought you could be spending your time in better ways. Whatever the reason, it was part of the work: to be new with everything. If you were completely present to whatever was happening, it could not be stale. Also, weren't we supposed to be beyond so many mind traps?

Although we were having some very dynamic classes, I noticed a new subtle flavor of irreverence sweeping the group. People were arriving late to class and carrying sodas and milkshakes from the burger joint next door. Some had an attitude in class like teenagers forced to do something uncool, and some people just stopped coming altogether. Something had changed. I couldn't put my finger on it, but a new energy was in the air. I had to take responsibility and see where I was not being new and fresh in this situation.

One night, Sarah was in the chair. She was a young and beautiful new devotee who was clearly in love with The Master. She seemed to worship him.

The class exercise that night was about "the man of salt." The visual was of a man made of salt. When he returns to the ocean, he returns to his true nature and dissolves. In doing this, he merges with the divine essence, which was his essence all along. While in the chair that night, Sarah began to profess her love for Andreas in her flowery way as she shared what she saw in the exercise. As the man of salt, obviously referring to Andreas, she walked into the ocean, eagerly following him. It was obvious that she saw him as her savior and her object of worship. Andreas was not merely a guru pointing the way up the mountain. But to her, he was the mountain. I thought, *Wasn't his role to show us the Christ within us, not see him as the Christ?*

At that point Nick, the most senior disciple, who always sat near Andreas, had a look of total disgust on his face. Then something completely unexpected happened.

"THIS HAS GOT TO STOP!" Nick roared into the room. He slapped his hands loudly on the floor and began to explain how this bowing down to Andreas, the man, was not what we were meant to be doing here. I agreed with Nick, but was still shocked by his strong reaction. What we did not know at the time was that he was also referring to Andreas' sexual behavior, which Nick found unacceptable as well.

Then, a reality-show drama began unfolding in rapid time. Beatrice, the female senior disciple, began yelling at Nick for his disrespectful infraction. "WHO ARE YOU TO SPEAK LIKE THAT?" she shot back. This was unprecedented, and all hell broke loose. Nick and Beatrice went at each other, yelling accusations. Then, a close friend and roommate of Nick', Katrina, rose from the crowd to defend Nick. It had all the makings of a great catfight or a mud-slinging wet T-shirt contest. It got very heated. These were the top disciples in the "knowing," coming unglued. They were fighting to defend and protect something, even though it was not really clear what was behind such an eruption.

I felt a tremendous sadness at the state of affairs and knew that things were permanently changing. We all left that night shocked and dismayed at the turn of events. Also about this time, the young and beautiful devotee David mysteriously left the Buddha Field. Hardly anyone ever left the Buddha Field. If they did, it caused quite a stir. To leave, you were usually "completely deluded," according to Andreas. It came as a complete surprise, because David had been very close to Andreas and did a lot of direct service for him around the house. He had a beautiful girlfriend who looked like a young Sophia Loren. David left her too, and she was heartbroken. They seemed so in love and none of this made any sense.

Shortly after this, another very disturbing incident occurred. Someone named Jude, an old disciple from many years back, broke into Andreas' home and barged into the middle of a cleansing session between Andreas and a devotee. Jude threw some furniture, broke things, and threatened Andreas physically. He accused him of ruining people's lives, being a fraud, sexually abusing men, being a criminal, a fugitive and a manipulator who needed to be stopped. If Andreas didn't stop giving people cleansing sessions, Jude threatened, he would seek legal action to stop him.

No one talked to Andreas this way.

These sudden experiences shook everyone up. Andreas was attacked? His furniture was thrown around? He was threatened with physical violence? What was happening? It was just too absurd to imagine. It was like someone vandalizing a sacred place.

Tamara lived far south of town, and the ride to her house took at least thirty minutes. My mind was preoccupied as I was headed to a Sunday-night celebration. As we all squeezed into her living room, there was palpable tension in the air. There were just so many conflicting feelings swirling around in everyone's minds. How do we protect Andreas? What if Jude is right? What if we are all fools? Maybe Jude is just a crazy, violent sociopath. What if there is a public exposure of the entire Buddha Field? What is the real story between Andreas and Jude? What about the sexual abuse accusations? I had never been abused. Maybe this was a fabrication. Were people just unable to handle the fact that Andreas had sexual relationships? What was the truth?

It was a somber group as Andreas made his entrance and took his seat. I honestly didn't know if he was going to be embraced or rejected by everyone. We were all waiting to see where our leader was going to take us from here. He began to share. He began to cry. Not just cry, but weep. Andreas was weeping, a sight I never in a million years thought I would witness. That sight alone moved others to tears. He essentially shared that it was time for him to go. I was very moved, but I felt strangely liberated as well. This came as a surprise. I went home and I wrote a poem.

JESUS WEPT

Jesus wept
Of course he wept
For the seemingly impenetrable
Shroud of ignorance
My master wept
For the bleeding of his heart
And for all of humanity
For the revolution needing to happen
I wept
At the sight of my master weeping
Because in that instant my heart grew so big
I became the Buddha
I knew I had more than enough love
To share with him
I wept in celebration
Of all that I have become and unbecome
In his presence
Today I surrender to
This holiness I have become
I am the fruit of his labor
I am

Just when I thought nothing else could happen, the other shoe finally dropped. A new accusing e-mail was sent to everyone in the Buddha Field, and probably others in the community as well. Amazingly enough, I never received a copy of this because, apparently, I was not on the Buddha Field mailing list. This was fine with me, because I did not want to read it. I was not ready to read accusations that my spiritual master was a criminal and a fugitive.

According to those who saw it, there was a picture of Andreas, and the whole thing was written in a sort of criminal "wanted poster" style. The accusations were fierce. I wanted this whole thing to just go away. I felt removed from this drama because it was not my drama. Weren't we supposed to avoid getting caught up in other people's dramas? I was committed to living these teachings.

Andreas asked me to speak with my lawyer again. He began to call me frequently to confer with me about the latest legal counsel I was receiving on his behalf.

CHAPTER 26

Exodus

Andreas left.

I felt completely lost. It was as if someone very close to me had died, and I now had a huge empty hole in my life. I went into grief, feeling abandoned, and spiraled into depression. I was also confused about how I was supposed to feel about Andreas. It felt too intense to even begin to unravel this twisted knot of love, gratitude, disgust, and fear. If he really was guilty of everything he was accused of, and I still loved him anyway, what did that say about me? Should I hate him because he had supposedly hurt others, even though he had been only kind and loving to me? How would I know if the accusations were true or false? Was it easier to just stay in denial as the repercussions of his downfall were just too unimaginable? If I was no longer living a life of devotion, then what was my life about? What was I going to do? How would I operate without trying to get love? Who was going to save me from a life of mediocrity now?

His location was highly confidential information. He was gone. He had left in the middle of the night and taken his entourage with him. But it was a new and younger version of his entourage. The others had abandoned him. The people who he chose to go with him basically left their lives with only a moment's notice, never to return again. For these people, there was just enough time to throw a bag together and go. I imagined half-drunk cups of tea left sitting on their kitchen tables, still steaming. After they were gone, there was essentially no contact between any of them and those of us here in Austin.

I missed my old life, my schedule, and my friends. I missed the energetic transmission that had been my steady diet for years. We had completely been able to withdraw from mainstream life while still living normally. We were in the world but not of the world. He had created this for us, which is no easy feat. I knew I could never return to a conventional life. Besides, why would I want to?

After a few months, a member of his entourage came back to Austin with a videotaped message from Andreas.

"Giselle, would you show the video at your house?" Lucio asked me. After hesitating and not really knowing quite what to do, I agreed.

About forty people came. It was eerie, watching Andreas on a huge rented video screen share satsang in my living room. The videotape was of him, very tanned, sitting on a white sofa with lots of sunlight in the room. He shared as if nothing had really happened. Some people cried, others felt confused or turned off to the whole spectacle. I felt weird, like this was a creepy and unhealthy scene, certainly not how I wanted to receive satsang. The division was beginning in the group between those who were "still with Andreas" and those who no longer wanted to be involved.

For several months, I cried a lot. But mostly I just felt depressed. It's funny how it seemed that no one banded together in grief over the death of this so-called life. People did so privately and with a full range of feelings about the matter. I became very isolated from the others, as did many people. Suddenly we all had all a lot of free time. People didn't quite know what to do. Meditation was difficult. I felt everything spiraling downward.

QUICKSAND

Help I am sinking
In the quicksand of maya
Moving wickedly slow
And imperceptibly
My feet innocently stepped into it
My legs took root

And drew down
Into the pull of the earth
Where gravity is the natural law
Then my organs became entombed and dulled
All openings being sealed off
Arms flailing
Grasping
Which only quickens the descent
Until there are only
My crocodile eyes
Skimming the surface
Scanning the horizon
For the only thing that can pull me out
Your hand
But wait you say, it is my own hand I am reaching for
And somewhere I know that
Yet still I cry for
Your hand

One day, while watching an old movie at the Paramount Theater in downtown Austin, I got a call from Andreas. I snuck into an old theater office so I could hear him clearly. I started crying and let him know how lost everyone was feeling, especially me. I told him how meditation had become very difficult. His fatherly tone was reassuring, and he invited me to come see him.

"Really?" I answered. This was the last thing I ever expected.

"Yes, in a few weeks."

"Thank you so much. I'd love to come," I replied. I was shocked. Another poem came:

THE CALL

My liberation is eminent
But not yet
I thought I was in love
Until I received your call
Which threw me into true meditation
That delicious familiar vibration
That sweeps ME *away*
You see I can use everything
I've been given
But still I need you
To take me where I cannot go myself
That is all there is to it

CHAPTER 27

A Visit to the Fugitive Camp

True to his word, Barry called in a few weeks, on behalf of Andreas, for me to visit. Of course, no one could know where I was going and precautions had to be taken.

This will be interesting, I thought.

I drove four hours to a beach town on the Texas coast and arrived at night. I followed directions through an upscale resort-styled neighborhood near the water. As I entered the house, everyone was on the back deck overlooking the water, in high spirits. There was a flurry of activity as people buzzed around, just as they had always done around Andreas. I felt as though these people were having a party while everyone in Austin was suffering. They hadn't missed a beat.

Outside, the moon was bright over the ocean. My old friends! It was great to see them, even though there was a slight awkwardness to the reunion. I didn't quite know how to be in this situation, as I was one of the first to visit the relocated tribe. My good friend Barry beamed at me and grabbed me in the longest hug. Then he held my hands in his and gazed into my eyes.

"Giselle, this is what you have always been waiting for. It's your time." He spoke in a very motherly tone.

I wasn't sure what he could possibly mean.

"You know how you have always talked about serving The Master directly. Well, this is what's happening for you. That time is here." His eyes were questioning.

"Wow." That's all I could say. This was what I had been waiting for. But now it seemed like a trick. I didn't trust this turn of events. It felt like I was being enticed into some form of slavery.

A few minutes later, Andreas came out of his room wearing a T-shirt, shorts, and his ever-present brown slippers. He made a grand entrance as always. He walked to the middle of the two-story living room and stopped. Everyone froze dead in their tracks as he and I had open-eye meditation for about five long minutes. There was complete silence and stillness in the room. Everyone was giving us a private moment of reunion, yet they were all participating. Tears came to my eyes. It was actually the beginning of the rainy season for me, emotionally. I shed the kind of deep tears that come from an endless well of sadness. It was not for me to know their origin at this time, as my tears would continue to flow on and off for the next several months. All I knew at that moment was that I had a feeling something was not right.

That night, and every night thereafter, we had dinner together, followed by a small satsang among the small group. Andreas spoke mainly about the situation in Austin and about those who had turned their backs on him. He was distraught that so many believed the vicious lies and accusations in the now-infamous e-mail. I was surprised to hear his private thoughts, which were a rare outpouring, on the matter. I felt like I had arrived in the inner circle of the family, hearing very personal information.

I had no idea what the schedule would be like now. I don't know what I was thinking, but I didn't realize that I would be in service every moment. There was no time for oneself, which is the idea of selfless service. But I had never really lived it twenty-four hours a day. The schedule was intense for me, as I found it hard to make phone calls, do any personal shopping and, most importantly, get enough rest. I also wondered why it felt like I was gaining weight when I was dancing and swimming every day. My body was not happy. I think it was because we ate so late and did not get enough sleep. I also had never lived in a communal setting. It had been a long time since I had roommates. But I was there only for a week while my children were with their dad. This made the demanding lifestyle tolerable, at least for the time being.

After waking up and meditating for at least an hour, some of us met for dance class. Everyone in the house danced aerobically as a group to music in the living room, and then those of us who were ballet dancers had a ballet class led by Andreas. The class took place on the back porch under the blazing sun. Then there was a meditation walk where we had the chance to develop a keen awareness of the flowers and birds and the pulse of life in full swing. It was kind of an unspoken invitation to a few people, mainly those who had business to discuss with Andreas.

I can only imagine what we looked like, walking down the middle of the street—me in ballet tights—as Andreas led the pack. We had business to discuss because I was still talking to lawyers about how he could protect himself from the anonymous writer of the e-mail, who was still a threat to him. We also talked about the looming threat of Jude.

It was a warm humid day in this small coastal town of Corpus Christi where I had grown up. All the yards were thick green carpets of St. Augustine grass, some freshly mowed. The air was salty and windy, not breezy and pleasant. There were some palm and mesquite trees but very few shade trees, which seemed to magnify the sun. I had to fight the urge not to repress feelings from my childhood that this environment conjured. As we walked, the subject came up of where Andreas' next destination would be because, I was told, this location was a temporary one. It was in the works for him to move somewhere else, although the new site had not been decided. It would probably be far away, outside the United States.

"If we go, Giselle, I see you coming with us," Andreas said.

I certainly wasn't expecting this, and a mental wall shot up immediately. I thought about my children.

"What about my kids?" I replied.

"Well, they could come with us," he said. More walls shot straight up. They could not leave Austin as part of my divorce agreement. Also, I would never force my path on them. It was out of the question. Right there on the spot, I knew this was guidance I would never follow, and my mind was made up. It was one thing for me to leave town for a week at a time when the children were scheduled to be with their dad, but anything beyond that was never going to happen.

"You know, Giselle, your kids will be with you. You don't have to worry about that," he said.

"Well if they can't leave, and I leave anyway, how is that going to work?" I asked.

"Maybe you tell William you want to leave and take the kids with you. He will say *no*, but eventually he will say *yes* and the kids will come and live with you," he said. "You will just have to trust. You know you are meant to be with me," he concluded.

I wasn't buying it. I could never leave my kids, trusting that someday they would somehow come and live with me. Even if

Andreas could see into the future, it was a risk I would never take. I realized, at that moment, he was no longer my teacher. He was someone who wanted something from me—something I could never give. I had learned to trust my intuition and my instincts and to live in the moment. In this moment, my mind was clear and resolute. My children came first. The love I had for them was more pure, more pristine than anything in my life.

But I didn't let on that the decision to stay was already made in my heart. I remained quiet.

After the walk, we had lunch that was prepared by disciples doing kitchen service. The cooking was demanding because it included preparing lunches in Tupperware for the entire group, followed by an evening meal for twelve to sixteen people. And, as always, special meals were prepared for Andreas. All of this was done without a commercial kitchen. They had to depend on four burners, an oven, and household appliances. The kitchen took a beating.

After lunch, there were a few hours before the daily afternoon outing. You never knew where the outing was going to be. It could be swimming on the beach, a walk somewhere downtown—the mall, the park, a bookstore, the gym, or the grocery store. We had to be ready and prepared with all the right gear, should any of the above happen. We were never told ahead of time.

When Andreas was ready, he would walk out of his room and straight to the car. At that moment, everyone was expected to be ready as well. We usually traveled in a caravan of four or five cars. We did everything together as a group. No one had the choice to stay home and read a book. You were required to participate in every activity with the group. Otherwise you were not a "yes." You were not doing your service and not "going for it." Therefore, why were you there at all?

It's amazing how no one ever veered. But I was secretly driving off the road. If you were serving Andreas and living with him, the schedule was nonstop. Disciples could not be late for dance or for dinner. In order to keep up with this, people frantically ran around looking stressed out just trying to keep up. On the other hand, all Andreas had to do was show up. Everyone else had to show up *and* do all the service required for him. People had to cook, clean, organize, *and* perform their daily jobs outside of the group in order to receive income.

I was slowly beginning to see how crazy it all was. Most of the disciples wanted to be around The Master during every possible waking moment. But I found it extremely difficult for many reasons. I am an introvert and desperately missed time alone. I missed my own routine, working out when I had energy, eating what and when it was good for my body, being able to make phone calls and having my own schedule. But, as Andreas said, there was too much "self" if you were not able to serve constantly. " You cannot go to God on your own terms." That was the teaching he relied on to reinforce our commitment to him.

At a certain point during my time at the beach location, I felt as if we were living like fugitives. NO ONE could know where we were. I stayed only for periods under a week so I would not miss time with my kids. I was instructed to vacuum out the sand in my car before I got home so no one would know I had been at the beach. We were told to keep watch over our phone bills and credit card charges, as they could be traceable. In the house where Andreas was staying with his entourage, the dining room had become command central, with at least six computers crowding the dining room table. This is where everyone set up their personal computers, ran their own businesses, or did work for Andreas.

After the daily outing, he always had bodywork or a massage while everyone else frantically showered and prepared the evening meal. Sometimes I would shower with two or three girls at the same time because we had to hurry and be ready when Andreas was ready. Sometimes, I even thought nothing of hopping in the shower with one of the men to save time. When Andreas was ready to eat, we were all together, ready to join him for the evening meal.

There was usually conversation during dinner. Eventually, the subject focused on the latest news about the situation in Austin and how "deluded" everyone was becoming, one by one. There was talk about how devotees were getting "poisoned" by the few that were truly deluded. It was starting to feel like gossip and judgment about people's choices. What had made me feel like an insider was now making me feel petty and part of a group preoccupation with what everyone was still doing in Austin. This micro version of the Buddha Field seemed paranoid, and it was uncomfortable. It was clear how desperate this group was to find out who was truly devoted to Andreas. I could sense the obsession with who was "in" and who was "out," and this seemed to become even more important than the spiritual teachings we were supposedly all there to experience. I felt disgusted by the obsession with the political, and potentially the legal, situation. My suspicions that this was a cult began to deepen.

On my second trip to visit, an amazing thing happened. We had a knowing session. After ALL those years of endless talk and speculation about the knowing, who had it, when there would ever be another session, who would get it, and who would be able to ask for one, I was chosen. Though I privately began to believe I was in a cult, there was still a large part of me who believed I could discern between teachings that were not authentic, and those with hidden and powerful potential. It was the promise of enlightenment that kept me there. And tonight would be big. It had been almost fifteen years since the last knowing session, and many believed Andreas would never grant one again.

The session took place in the living room. As usual, everything began with dinner, followed by satsang. We didn't have a clue when it was going to happen, so we had no expectations going in. The lights were dimmed, and Andreas announced that some of us were ready to receive the knowing, just like that. Not everyone in the room that night received it, but there would be other nights to follow. But on that night, I was one of the first to receive it. As he called me up, I felt like an innocent child, not knowing what was going to happen. As I knelt before him, Andreas placed his hands on my head. He took his time, and I felt another channel opening inside me. He guided me through the short process and revealed the experience of light. My entire world opened up. I will tell you about the experience in present tense because, to me, I am still living it:

I feel as if I am moving forward in space or being sucked into a tunnel only to be spit out at the other end, floating in space. It's as if I am allowed to view something new. I have no control, and it is different every single time. Sometimes absolutely nothing happens, just empty dark space. Sometimes a pin of light appears that grows and draws me in. Sometimes there is a brilliant flash of light, white hot. Sometimes there are fireworks of light and outer-space scenes, as if universes are being born. It feels like viewing creation.

An energy, or a state of being, comes with it. I can also describe it as a suspended form of exaltation. I am floating in a divine current or vibration, losing the smaller self and being merged with the big self. That is all there is.

This was and is my experience. Here I was, undeniably receiving something amazing from someone who I was beginning to distrust. This was hard to reconcile. The experience was amazing, but the whole organization was becoming increasingly unsettling.

After the initiation and a very long period of this newly revealed meditation that went well into the early morning hours, we walked outside. It was four in the morning, but the moon brightly lit the sky. Everything, even in the dark, was vibrantly alive. Words failed me. All I could say was that I felt like I was on an acid trip. I remember staring at a bush, and above it was the moon. We were all so intimate: the moon, the bush, everything and me in this heightened awareness. After this trip, I was driven home transformed once again to my life in Austin.

I returned to Andreas again, but only for a few days. After ballet class on the porch in the morning, I went on the walk to discuss some Buddha Field business. On this particular morning, we talked about the logistics of Andreas' move. Then the subject came up once again about whether or not I was going to join him.

"I'm concerned about my kids," I blurted out. But before he could even finish his sentence, I felt the hair rising on my back at the thought of him once again suggesting I go. The conversation was a replay of our earlier one involving me moving with him. Again, he suggested I leave my kids, trusting that my ex-husband would eventually hand them over.

I knew my answer was a resounding *no,* but I still felt as though I might not be "choosing the highest." Strangely, I was still not ready to walk away completely and leave his company. I had become hooked on my deepening experience and the belief that I needed Andreas to make it happen. I had bought into his talk that walking away from the group was a form of delusion and that I would lose the protective shield of grace that came with being with a master.

CHAPTER 28

*Gypsy Camp leaves
the Mainland*

Not too long after this trip, Andreas and his entourage prepared to leave. The gypsy camp would disappear soon to a new location. Weeks were spent researching new locations and real-estate rentals. The move would be intense, although the only baggage would be clothes for the disciples and all of Andreas' personal items, including his chair, his bed, and his reading table. A car was purchased that was the exact make and model of his current car, which had to be customized and sent to the new location in advance. This was actually a weeks-long process of finding and retrofitting a seat to his liking. Someone actually made wooden mock-ups of the inside of the car so he could it try out. His body was "easily thrown out" and "extremely sensitive," so he could sit comfortably only in *his* chair, ride in *his* car, and sleep in *his* bed, no exceptions.

Unbeknownst to him, I was going to accompany them for about a week and help them get settled. Even though I had doubt, I feared leaving the group and losing all the spiritual ground I had made. Or worse, I feared regressing into my previous state of being—asleep. As luck would have it, the flight fell on a week that I didn't have the kids. I booked my flight so that I met up with the group while they were on a layover, midway to the final destination. There they all were, walking silently behind Andreas, traipsing through the airport.

When Andreas saw me, he walked over, and we held each other's gaze. I could tell he was glad I was there. I spoke with Barry to let him know that I was there just for a week, helping with the move, and then heading back home. I felt compelled to help Andreas because I was still too afraid of disappointing my father figure, once again. Besides, my mother had taught me how to stick with someone even if you're miserable. I was also attached, unhealthy as it was, to living a life of complete devotion. It was my identity.

Barry relayed my sentiments to Andreas. There was never a big discussion about my not moving to the new location, but the information was simply passed along. I sat directly behind Andreas on the flight over. It was a long journey and, after positioning Andreas perfectly in his seat, the disciples meditated the entire time.

After arduous travel, we ventured out to see the island. It was beautiful. I felt like everything transformed from black-and-white to Technicolor. This was Oz.

Andreas' house was a rental in a very nice neighborhood populated with a few Hollywood stars who vacationed there occasionally. The space was decorated in a beautiful contemporary style, with a metal gate at the driveway and lushly landscaped grounds. The kitchen had new granite countertops. And from the windows and balcony, you could see the tranquil turquoise water licking the edge of the pristine beach. The house had three bedrooms upstairs, a master suite downstairs, and another living area off the master suite. This is where we gathered.

Within no time, the schedule was the same and everything was in its place, thanks to the expertise of the crew. They were extremely competent and served selflessly. We started to explore the natural and beautiful surroundings a little more each day. We went for swims in the ocean and took nature walks. The new location seemed to suit everyone. Then, as quickly as I came, I left.

Back in Austin, I was grateful to be in my "comfortable" life at home with my kids. My experience with Andreas had taken me deeper once again, but it seemed like every time I had such an experience, a counter-effect would soon follow. As far from the mind as I had been, I seemed to snap back into the world quickly. Soon after my return, I found myself looking for excitement—good, fleshy, earthy, sensual, physical-world excitement. The old-fashioned kind. My senses were more alive than ever.

At Whole Foods one day, I stood in the checkout line, devouring all the gossip magazines. Being a closet trash-magazine junkie, I allowed myself to read them only in line and did not buy them. They were always an escape and a distraction for me. This was at the height of Brad Pitt and Angelina Jolie's love affair. Skimming the highlights of their jet-setting global lifestyle, I had a little thought. "Wouldn't that be fun? To be a part of a glamorous couple that traveled around the world and did humanitarian work in the process?" And then I forgot about it. But the order had been placed. That's how it works. We always get what we want, and we have to very specific in the orders we place with the universe.

The following evening I went to a friend's yoga class, followed by a trip to the raw food bar back at Whole Foods. I was sitting at the bar was my friend and fellow devotee, Roberto, who also happened to be one of Andreas' principal body workers. I had not seen him in a while, and we caught up. As I was ready to leave, he stood up and put his hands in the air.

"Wait just three more minutes. There's a friend I want you to meet," he said with a smile. *Hmmm*, I thought. Roberto had a devilish look on his face and was having fun with this mischievous moment.

"No, I really need to go," I said. But I was very curious and loved surprises.

"Come on, Giselle, he's already here. He's just looking for a parking space, and he'll be here in a second," he pleaded.

CHAPTER 29

The Sighting

Before I could even respond, Joaquin came sauntering toward us.

"Joaquin!" I excitedly called out. Then I did something I have never done, especially to a six-foot-two grown man. I ran up to him, grabbed him around the waist, picked him up, and twirled him around the floor in the middle of the store. He was as surprised as I was at my behavior. Didn't I have any cool? But I wasn't thinking. It was an innocent reaction to being glad to see him. At the time, it was hard to compose myself or contain my joy.

So Joaquin suddenly reentered my life. He was sexy, charming, flamboyant, mysterious, dangerous, adventurous, romantic, and seductive. He was a sight for my sore eyes. It had been about a year or more since I had seen him, and he had just flown in from Europe. The timing was perfect.

I was hesitant about jumping into anything romantically, especially with someone who looked a little too good to be true. I wasn't too sure about this mysterious character. Nick had said to me that if I ever hung out with a guy like that, he would never speak to me again. I wasn't sure what he meant by "a guy like that." All I knew was that Joaquin looked like a ruggedly handsome rock star. He was tall, with a bold head and a prominent brow line. He had a wild mane of hair, the body of a college quarterback (and he moved like one), with a big wide grin. He reminded me of Steven Tyler. He also possessed an intoxicating energy, sexual magnetism, eloquence, a great sense of humor, and Texas charm. To top it off, he traveled around the world as an entrepreneur, mostly living in Europe and Asia. I remembered the order I had placed with the universe and considered it delivered.

"Do you want to do something tonight?" he asked. It was clear to me that he wanted to find out if I was single.

"Maybe tomorrow night," I suggested. He agreed. The next night I went on my ritual Barton Springs swim, even though it was winter. I used a wetsuit, but I could feel the freezing-cold water through the second skin. I finished up quickly and threw on some jeans so I could meet Joaquin for dinner. I wasn't trying to impress him, which was not my usual style. Usually, I would spend a good amount of time primping and getting ready. Instead, we met at the pool, and I was a mess. I decided that we should go to Curra's because I had a craving for their hot *caldo* after my brisk winter swim. But Joaquin did not like the food or the restaurant at all. He preferred fish and vegetables—all the time. Afterwards, we went to Truluck's downtown for a decadent dessert called "chocolate in a bag," which was actually a bag made out of chocolate, filled with a combination of delectable chocolate treats. It was the first sip of wine and the first taste of chocolate I had had in many years. I thought that indulging could be a "slippery slope." Then we kissed. In the restaurant. And it was amazing. Afterward, we talked and flirted in the car. We knew, without daring to say a word, there would be a great adventure in store for us. We made a date for the following night. It lasted two weeks. The third date lasted almost three. Then he left to travel, and I left to tend to my dying father.

CHAPTER 30

A Lovely Death

The idea of going to my small hometown of Sealy, Texas, for an indefinite amount of time and watching my father die sounded like a prison sentence.

"Go and be of assistance," Andreas advised by telephone. He worked with people who were "dropping their bodies" and assisted them in passing over through the Bardo, the astral plane where souls tend to get stuck after dying. He always lovingly told us to look for him when we were dropping our bodies and he would be there, absolutely.

"Be my hands," were Andreas' words to me as I prepared to enter the psychological puzzle known as my parents' home. They were both raised in this rural Texas town by Germanic parents who emphasized hard work, sacrifice, keeping problems private, and the belief that marriage was an obligation. Consequently, I had spent many years learning how to feel my feelings. I only knew how to express them artistically, not emotionally.

My father and I had problems, but we did have a deep bond. I had something to offer him on his journey toward physical death. Andreas had taught us that we were the potentiality of Buddha and had much to offer the people in our lives through being present in "shakti breath."

My father had been battling bone cancer for a decade, always beating it with the latest experimental therapy. We called him the "comeback kid" because he had reached the end many times only to come back a survivor. Of course, the subject of my father had come up many times in cleansing with Andreas, and it was an important relationship for me to heal in this lifetime. I would ask Andreas, every time things looked for my dad as if "this was it," if it was time yet for me to go and be with him for the last few weeks of his life. Every single time, the answer was, "No, he's not going anywhere yet," or "He still has time." But this time when I called Andreas, the answer was different.

"It would be good to go and see him," he suggested. I had to go.

By the time I arrived, my father was small and gray and helpless like a baby. My mother was a saint who took care of his every need, keeping him comfortable in the hospital bed that had been installed in their bedroom. But despite the grimness of this hospice environment, there was love in the air. A tenderness had come over the house that I had never experienced there before. There was nothing to do but meditate and wait for him to occasionally open his eyes so that whoever was there could speak lovingly to him.

After four days, I began feeling restless and needed organic food to replenish my body. I wanted to make a trip back to Austin for supplies, but Andreas strongly advised against it. My rebellious nature was really spiked in this home environment, so I decided to go anyway. I was risking not being there when he passed, but I just had to do it. I came back as soon as I could and settled in for the duration.

Once I surrendered and made myself completely in service to the situation, everything changed. I was speaking to and being guided by Andreas daily, and I was beginning to really connect with my father in a way I never had before. We didn't speak, though we communicated with energy and our eyes. I saw him, and he saw me. When I had his conscious attention I would let him know how loved he was and how there was nothing to be afraid of. It was OK to let go. He would struggle and tell me how he wanted to have everything taken care of for my mother before he went and how he worried about her. I reassured him that there was nothing to be done other than to relax. Everything was already taken care of.

His lucidity was becoming less frequent, although there were some extremely bright moments when he would abruptly open his eyes and look into mine. I started to tell him to go toward the light. Andreas told me that my father was seeing his mother, his sister, and his daughter (my sister), standing at the foot of the bed, helping him. When I asked if he could see them, he just looked in their direction as if he was looking at them. He was halfway between this world and the next. His body was becoming weaker. There is no greater moment of compassion for the frailty of the human body than witnessing your mother changing your father's diapers. My once-emotional-abuser had become a child.

For whatever doubt I was having about Andreas and the Buddha Field, I could not have been a source of comfort and light for my parents without his guidance. Along with my mother, we were able to bring peace and a sense of dignity to an otherwise discouraging situation. Experiences like these kept me hooked into Andreas' teachings, though I knew I would eventually depart. There are beginnings and there are endings. Maybe they were the same. As I began helping my father transition from his physical body, my life was changing too.

I was assisting my father in leaving his body, directed by Andreas. I was helping my father to move out of his physical body by providing the loving energy of shakti. Sometimes we have trouble letting go of our bodies, a process that happens over several days—you usually don't simply slide out. I would alternately place my hands on his feet and head. Then I would open myself up to allow loving divine energy and assistance to flow through. I did this for several days.

One morning my mother said, "I think it's time." A hospice worker had told us that many dying people wait for everyone to leave the room at the moment of death. I went in, held his hand, and told him I loved him and to go toward the light. He acknowledged he heard me, then Mother and I both left.

A few minutes later, the hospice caregiver returned only to say, "He's gone." At that time, I offered my assistance to help his bodily exit by touching him again and transferring shakti energy. We waited for my other sister to come, and then we made the call to the funeral director. Mother went into busy mode, and I stayed with my father's body. I left the room to speak to Andreas on the phone and when I returned, the funeral director was already there, removing the body.

"Wait! I want to say good-bye!" I said to the small crowd gathered.

"They are taking the body, Janis!" my mother asserted, since the "authorities" had now taken over.

"No. Everyone please leave and give me some time," I demanded. I know I was making my mother feel very uncomfortable, as she liked to follow procedures. But I was able to finish the assistance as was directed, much to the confusion of everyone waiting on me and wondering, "What is she doing in there with the body?"

After much activity, arrangements, and crying from everyone, it was time for the funeral. The church was completely full, which surprised me. You could hear a pin drop. I had invited

William, my ex-husband, whom my mother adored. He sat with the family, and I was surprised at how much he cried. I loved him more in that moment, seeing his heart wide open. I hadn't seen that part of William in a long time. I felt like he was crying for many reasons. It was such an expansive moment.

Several old friends and wartime buddies of my father offered eulogies. When the preacher asked if anyone else wanted to eulogize, I stood up. It wasn't what anyone expected, including me. It didn't matter that I did not know what I was going to say. But years of class had taken away any fear of speaking to large groups. It was virtually impossible for me to be humiliated. But it was more than that. I had to share what I was feeling—an overwhelming, unconditional divine love for everyone present. My emotions poured out of me like a fountain. It was the most natural thing to stand up and let it flow out into the room.

I looked at the congregation, and I would not trade what I saw at that moment for anything. I saw a church packed with people who looked like children, who were forced to confront their greatest fear: death. They were innocent and raw in the unknowingness of death. Then I saw the front row of pallbearers, large Texas-size men who were crying like babies, also confronting their fears and their feelings. It was absolutely gorgeous. I was witness to the beautiful vulnerability of the human race. I felt only compassion, no judgment, as we were all one. It was love itself asking for love and receiving love.

Somehow, I got out of the way and my larger self began to speak. Looking back, I realize that it didn't matter what I said. But it was the vibration that I was experiencing that communicated more than words ever could.

"The other day, I was sitting with my dad and the room was cold. I reached out for his hand to hold. 'Let me warm your hand,' I said as I took his hand in mine. He opened his eyes and looked at me and released his hand from inside mine and instead wrapped his hand around mine, to warm *me* up. He didn't say a word. And in that moment, everything changed for both of us."

Then I continued to talk about how so much love was flooding through that a whole lifetime of deep wounds were healed. He finally had a chance to express his tender love and care, and I finally was able to gratefully receive it. This moment said everything—how he was sorry for not being there for me, how much he loved me, how he did the best he could and more. All the stories of this life were dissolved in love. My great neglector became pure and innocent love as we forgave each other for everything.

Death was a very popular subject of study in the Buddha Field, as it is in all great spiritual traditions. We were frequently taught to practice dying to all that is false. Once you learn to die to all that is false, you transcend death and realize that death is an illusion, just like the physical body is an illusion. Even knowing that there is no death, I was astounded at the power of it. I saw my father let go toward the light. He did not turn away from it. I know that so much was healed in that instant and that we were both transformed in a way I still cannot explain. I guess if you can't explain it, you got it. What I had dreaded so much had turned out to be one of the most exquisite heart-openings in this life. I can see how people are drawn to the service of hospice work.

According to Andreas, this was a turning point for me, and an initiation into a new realm. I felt it. Once again, my vibration had been recalibrated.

CHAPTER 31

A Trip Around the World

True to the pendulum swing of expansion and contraction, it was high time for another date with Joaquin. After saying "good-bye" to one physical form, I was ready to say "hello" to another in a very physical way. I was ready for the flesh experience. Our next date lasted six weeks and circled the globe completely.

We snuggled cozily into our airline seats and flew into the sunset on our way to Amsterdam. When you fly into the sun, it sets for hours. Outside our plane window was the surreal show of a luminous liquid sunset in iridescent colors of peach, indigo, gold, lavender, and every shade in between. Such a magnificent display was a good sign that the trip was going to be a great adventure.

I had always wanted to go to Europe, not as a tourist, but on a true adventure. I had also always wanted to go on a whirlwind, deliriously happy European honeymoon while madly in love. Well, most of my desires truly lined up for this one.

I had primarily stayed home for the past thirteen years with children, and I was ready to be out in the world again. Before this, I had never wanted to leave the children for more than a week. But with Joaquin, I was ready for this journey.

We were drunk on happiness, even though we were severely jet-lagged when we arrived in Amsterdam on a bright morning. After settling in, Joaquin drove me around on the back of a bicycle we bought from a junkie, which he had stolen and which was promptly stolen from us. We then rented another one and saw the city, meeting up with old friends of his. Joaquin knew the city well. I was very impressed by the transportation system, the architecture from the medieval to the present, the quality of the design, the infrastructure, the organic food, and the awareness of the people. The entire society seemed highly intelligent. There was a sharpness, an openness, a presence to everyone. People connected with you through their eyes. And everyone seemed to be in love. But the outer always reflects the inner. I was in love, so maybe it seemed like everyone around me was in love, too.

At sunset, everyone unwound from the day by gathering in the outdoor bars and cafés strewn along the canals. From our vantage point, I saw gorgeous Dutch women who, wearing thigh-high boots, drove up on motorcycles. They took off their helmets while shaking out their beautiful hair. I was blown away by their natural beauty.

We rented a small apartment at a beautiful place called "True Love." And, true to our place, we woke up every morning by making love until we were too hungry to do anything else but go out to eat. We practiced the yogic exercises known as the Tibetan Rites together while the sun poured in through the windows like honey. We went out for omelets and big bowls of cappuccino. We met his ruggedly beautiful and sexy Spaniard friend, Toron the painter, for drinks. In the evening we went to the sauna, an old art deco architectural masterpiece, and scrubbed our naked bodies. We went to the outdoor market and bought Tuscan lamb shearling coats from Italy. We went to the cosmopolitan stores and bought tight jeans for next to nothing. The Hari Krishnas danced through town, and I joined in for a while. Joaquin and I had the most romantic dinner ever. Our wineglasses shone with the same exquisite light we had just seen in Vermeer paintings at the Reichs Museum. We went to the LeidsePlein late at night and ate waffles that were really crepes, piled high with whipped cream and strawberries. We bought Stroup waffles from candy vendors on the canals.

We walked everywhere holding hands. We crashed a party at the Embassy and snuck into private quarters. We strolled into movie theaters looking for movies in English. We rode bikes through the fairytale environment of Wunderkind Park and its butterscotch lighting. We went to the coffee shops and read the exotic menus for marijuana like "Laughing Buddha" or "Blueberry Fields Forever." We strolled the red light district and talked to the girls that worked there. We were invited to join a few of the girls as a couple.

All the while I was enjoying this, I could hear Andreas' voice inside my head. "Giselle, you are not just taking a trip, you are really on a trip. Why do you need to travel? There is no there, there. How many lifetimes are you going to do this? Don't get distracted. Watch your escapist tendencies. You will never be fulfilled by a man. What are you serving right now? Who is your master? Don't miss this lifetime. You have great periods of insight, and then you get lured back into the world. Who's the one who needs to travel? Total surrender equals total freedom."

The fact was, I was supposed to be joining Andreas in Hawaii. He was expecting me. And I was planning to go. I was just taking the long way around the globe. Joaquin and I were both meditating every morning, and I was trying to keep up my evening meditations. But, as Andreas had said, there were some fierce distractions. Joaquin and I were both reading *The Power of Now* by Eckhart Tolle wherever we went. In some ways, Joaquin's master was the "now." Because those of us in the Buddha Field were told to stay away from spiritual books except those recommended by Andreas, I felt like I was betraying him. But the more I read, the more I realized that this book was a living, breathing fountain of truth. Every word was infused with direct knowledge of consciousness and presence. One only needed to choose a random page to be thrown back into the sweet arms of presence. Anytime or anywhere.

It was hard for Joaquin to accept the fact that I had a master, even though he had met Andreas and been touched by his brief encounter with the Buddha Field. It was one thing to be touched by Andreas, and it was another thing to have to compete with him for my attention. Being a man's man from Texas, this just didn't sit well with Joaquin. He didn't like the way I dropped everything when Andreas called, or the way I would speak to him only privately. This drove him crazy, but I could not share my heart with Andreas with Joaquin listening. He wanted me to put him on speakerphone, which I found to be unacceptable. But in wisdom and fairness, Joaquin did not press the issue. He knew what he was getting into with me, and he respected my decision. He also knew that he could not force anything on me. And if he tried, it would drive me away. But the more we became a couple, the more it became an issue.

Joaquin felt like I had a unique relationship with Andreas and like I was his "favorite" and therefore "allowed" to do whatever I wanted. The perspective of an insider like me never matched the perspective of an outsider. I never saw it that way, because there was no hierarchy. Instead, I saw Andreas having the relationship that was needed with each individual devotee.

After playing in Amsterdam, it was time for Joaquin to go to work. We boarded a train, which is my very favorite way to travel, for Switzerland. Just slide on, slide on the luggage, enjoy the ride, slide through the country, and then slide off. We moved into a '60s-style vintage rock hotel in the old part of Zurich with cobblestone streets. I accompanied Joaquin to his meetings with business associates while we created new opportunities as well. Some of the meetings were on Lake Zurich in a beautiful old restaurant, named Terrase, filled with wealthy citizens from all over the globe. Some of them brought their dogs in tow, looking like old-world aristocrats.

The sensory orgy continued. In Switzerland, there was CHOCOLATE. And croissants. There was the vibrantly alive farmer's market inside the grand Zurich train station, with homemade sausages from local farmers and rows and rows of expensive mushrooms. And all this sprawled under a three-story live Christmas tree dripping in Swarovski crystals! It was truly breathtaking. We looked for apartments in ancient buildings that transported you back to another century. I swam naked among many naked locals in the freezing lake at the outdoor spa on "women only" day.

I avoided calling Andreas because I did not want to commit to when I would arrive in Hawaii. Joaquin and I had just begun our adventure. In fact, we were just getting started. And I also did not want any guidance on my trip or my relationship. I had a range of emotions that went from feeling that I was a disobedient child, to fear that I was missing my chance for enlightenment and had sold out for worldly pursuits. But my experience with Joaquin was innocent like a child—in love, relaxed, and experiencing so much beauty.

My children were prepared for me to be gone only three weeks. We were in communication, but I know they were really missing me, and I missed them.

We left Switzerland and took a train to the Italian Alps for pristine snow and perfect skiing conditions. We stayed in an Austrian village and found a quaint restaurant where we ate every single night. As usual, Joaquin befriended the chef, so we never ordered. We would arrive and then were served course after course of incredible French food. Each night the chef would try and impress us more, which he did. During those dinners we talked for hours about everything and endlessly amused each other. We saw a religious rite on the day of Lent Procession, which consisted of all the men in the village wearing black, walking through the village. I saw my first real castle, mounted up on a high hill overlooking the village.

From there we flew to Dubai on an amazing airline that felt like a private jet. The service was first class and the music was intoxicating. The inside of the plane was done in soothing pastel sunset colors, and the attendants were beautiful. I did not want this "bubble of pink luxury" flight to end. The city itself was exploding with industrious energy. There was a forest of skyscrapers under construction. We stayed just as long as it took to have some meetings, and then we were off to Southeast Asia.

Landing in Manila was an abrupt change from the refinement of Europe and the Middle East. Hello, third-world country. The heat and humidity were overwhelming, the airport was a zoo, and the whole city was crammed with people. There were too many cars, too much pollution, too much karaoke noise, and too much survival energy. It had its own fascination.

The people in Manila were very service-oriented. We found a moderate hotel, which I later found out was a brothel. Obviously, it was very good at being discrete. This city seemed to be stuck in the second chakra. Everything had a sexual vibe to it or, rather, a sexual obsession. There were many transsexual and transgender men who looked remarkably like women. I quit trying to guess, because I was always wrong. Many of these men were prostitutes. According to some, heterosexual men hire these men who look like women for sex. This is not considered gay behavior in Manila.

I finally took the plunge and called Andreas. I told him I was on my way, and he asked about my relationship with Joaquin. He then told me that, psychologically, I just wanted to *be* Joaquin, since my father had wanted me to be a boy. This actually hit home, even though I didn't want to admit it. The one thing I could never be was the son my father always wanted. Andreas told me that Joaquin had nothing to offer me and that the treasure he was looking for was not buried in the earth. One thing is for sure—Joaquin and I were both digging for treasure of one sort or another.

Just one of Joaquin's entrepreneurial ventures is digging for gold. Seriously. There is known gold buried by Yamashito during World War II in the Philippines. There are literally tons of gold that have not been accounted for, which can be located by advanced technological equipment.

He had a dig site with known treasure for years, but could not recover it. This made no sense to me. How hard can it be to dig up the earth and get it out? Well, you would be surprised. One of the many difficult factors was that it was buried with the intention of never being found or recovered—unless you were the ones burying it. In fact, it was so secret, many of the men digging the holes were buried alive in order to keep it hidden. A corps of Japanese engineers spent years on each burial site planting traps, some with poisonous gases and underground mazes. Some of the traps were filled with water so that if it was hit, that tunnel would be flooded out.

The dig sites were tricky to locate. Everyone in the Philippines knew where buried treasure was, and for a small fee could take you to the "real sites." And once you did find a real one, they were hard to reach. This required negotiation with the landowner and finding competent diggers. *Competent* is the key word here. The sites had to be kept secret, which was next to impossible. You had to have a driver who served as a bodyguard and who, hopefully, was a hired policeman and could carry a gun. Basically, this person would have a license to kill. Treasure hunting could only occur during those months of the year when it was not rainy season plagued by typhoons. You had to figure out a way to get the gold out once you found it, out of the ground, off the site, and out of the country, because it was illegal to take treasure. Therefore, no one dug with a permit. These are just a few of the minor challenges of digging for treasure in the Phillipines. And this is why you could dig at one site for years with no recovery.

At one point, Joaquin got a tip from his driver about a site (everyone wanted to sell you a site map) that looked good. The only drawback was that it was buried next to a huge dump site that was at least ten stories high. And if that wasn't enough, the site was under a running creek bed. This is the part of the book where I would consider adding photos, because you just have to see it to believe it.

As we drove up, I was shocked to see the largest and tallest dump site I could ever imagine. The scale was monumental, at least seven stories tall, and went on for many hectares. Getting out of the van, I expected to be hit with the putrid smell of waste and decay. However, once I let go of the conditioned response, the smell was actually sweet. There were flies engulfing the van, but as we hiked up the mountain of trash, they thinned out. We walked on everything a human could discard in the twentieth century. It was an archaeological anthology of our world. We ascended one side and scaled down the slippery slope of the back side. This was quite a challenge because *you did not want to fall down*. That was unthinkable, although it wasn't as slimy as

I would have thought. In fact, there was a beauty to it. If you forgot what the mind had to say and dropped all judgment, it was magnificent. And then there was the added danger of local, self-appointed guerilla soldiers, equipped with machine guns, policing the area. The agreement was that we were under their protection in exchange for a piece of the action. The truth was that they would have killed us in an instant, and we were never going to share the gold.

The colors, the textures, the oddest collection of objects were thrown into bizarre random arrangements. At one point, I noticed actual totems constructed from the debris by an anonymous trash artist. I was in awe of the relentless pursuit of beauty under the most dire conditions. It was a proud human moment, and I felt like I had entered a Jackson Pollock painting.

Every now and then, as I looked down and negotiated each step, smoke rose. At first, I thought the mountain was burning, but then I realized it was decomposing. The whole mountain was smoldering with decay. If we waited long enough, we could dig for diamonds.

The site was next to a beautiful creek with black water running through it. There was a textile manufacturer upstream, and every day the water was a different color, depending on the dye being used. It was tragic to see children playing in this water as if they were in some crystal-clear swimming pool. At the "X marks the spot" dig site, I climbed down in the hole as Joaquin coached me through my claustrophobia. There was actually a digger in this tiny space, way under the earth with a flashlight, a hammer, and a chisel, digging away. I cannot imagine doing that job every day for months at a time.

As fascinating as this was (and it was) I was beginning to feel a pull to go and see Andreas. It was getting time to continue moving around the other side of the globe. I made preparations to leave as Joaquin made preparations to stay and buy more powerful equipment for the dig. It was time.

I flew business class, which felt like the height of luxury after being in the Philippines. When I finally landed on the island where Andreas was living, I did not announce my arrival. Instead, I checked into a hotel and slept off jet lag for two days. I was not ready to dive into full service.

I moved into the "helper" house with about six devotees who lived there permanently. It was communal living, which I found to be conducive to inner work. We were all silent most of the time and respectful of each other's things and space. The house felt like an ashram because we were all focused on meditation and service. I was actually surprised by how much I liked it. Maybe it was because I knew that I was a short-timer. Also, it was easy to get along because we were constantly doing service or going on outings.

Our daily schedule consisted of meditation at the house first thing in the morning, dance at his house, a walk, and then a lunch break. After a few "free" hours—which were really filled with service like shopping or cleaning (sometimes I sewed for him)—there was an outing somewhere on the island. Snorkeling, hiking, or swimming got us home way after dark. Then, while Andreas had his bodywork done, we all took speedy showers so we would be seated and ready when he came out for dinner. Next, we all shared over dinner, then watched an hour or two of television. Sometimes we would watch *Nip and Tuck* or *Family Guy*. The show was always Andreas' selection. This was followed by hours of meditation until about one or two in the morning, or even longer. Then we would drive home for sleep, which was never enough.

"You don't have to go around the world to get to the other side of the mountain," were his first words to me as we were seated for dinner my first night back.

"Yes, but it sure was fun," I said. It was not a very spiritual answer.

"So what did you see out there?" Andreas responded.

"I saw lots of beauty, and had many moments of...." I trailed off with my response as I noticed he was not really looking at me, but straight ahead and speaking in a very monotone voice.

"Uh huh," he said as he picked up the remote and started scrolling through the channels, obviously ignoring me.

I felt dismissed, discounted, and judged. It felt as though my beautiful trip and my romantic relationship didn't count. I felt like a child bursting through the front door to tell her parent about the most exciting day of her life, only to have the door slammed in her face. This was Andreas' way of communicating to me and the group that my worldly experiences were unimportant, something I had seen him do many times to others. I was being punished as an example of a deluded escapist. This was communicated without his saying a word, as his voice had now become the voice in my own head. This was also the childhood neglect that was so painfully familiar to me.

My visit was short and sweet, because I had spent all my time in Europe and I needed to get back to my family. I returned to Texas and a warm homecoming, and was very excited to see the kids. Lying in bed one night, I got an unexpected call from Andreas. He wanted to strongly recommend a book called *Rajarsi Janakananada* by Yogananda's first spiritual successor. I actually had that book from years ago and had previously read it. It is the story of one of Yogananda's chief disciples, a man named Mr. Lynn, who becomes enlightened in a very short period of time. It is the beautiful account of a master/disciple relationship. It actually turns into a deep friendship as well, and includes personal correspondence between the two. During one of Yogananda's trips back to India, Mr. Lynn, a very wealthy and astute businessman, took it upon himself to buy a valuable piece of the California coastline. He then proceeded to develop and build a center for Yogananda, and it eventually became the Center for the Society for Self-Realization.

I was surprised at Andreas' blatant agenda. I didn't respond. After we hung up, it was clear that he viewed me as a potential financial savior and patron to his own monument. This was a role I was not willing to assume.

CHAPTER 32

Hawaii

For Christmas that year, I decided to take the kids and Mariela to the islands. I had no expectation of them meeting Andreas; I just wanted to share this beautiful island with them. I also knew I would be able to see Andreas, at least for a few evening satsangs. I rented a house for us right on the beach. It couldn't have been more idyllic. We awakened to the sound of the waves and distant voices. We walked outside and saw beautiful bodies surfing, rowing, swimming, snorkeling, running, tanning, embracing, windsurfing, cycling, and simply enjoying some of the most profound natural beauty this planet has to offer. We swam in turquoise waters outside the back door with giant sea turtles, beautiful coral, and brightly colored fish. I found it hard to show up for service every morning at Andreas' house as I just wanted to relax and soak up this magical spot with my family. So I mostly did.

Andreas telephoned first thing every morning to see how we were. One morning I told him that my son was not feeling well. He made a few suggestions and sent over his two personal body workers to help. They showed up in total service, ready to help. I watched as Pante gently used her hands on my son's stomach to help with his pain. After a time he appeared to be somewhat better. The other body worker, Oso, giggled with the kids. He was just a big kid himself.

There was a dance beginning to happen, and I knew that Andreas wanted to include the children. I was feeling like I was getting special attention, which I always liked. I was hopeful that my children could meet Andreas. I longed for my two worlds to come together, the two most important things to me: my children and my path to awakening.

The children and Mariela met Andreas in a very low-key setting on the beach during sunset one night. He walked up to us with his entourage, then stepped right up to each child, without saying a word, and gazed into their eyes. Neither one looked away but instead looked right back at him as if it was the most natural thing in the world. I had told them about Andreas by this point, so they were very curious.

I found myself once again in a profoundly beautiful setting, where everything on the outside is perfect. I have experienced this many times in my life. However, once again, there was something wrong. I simply could not stop crying. It started one day. I was not sobbing, but tears just started leaking out of me. And they came and came and came most of the day. But I had to continue my day and let them come. My weather was definitely cloudy and rainy, with a steady downpour. The tears came from a deep well of sadness that I could not put my finger on. I stopped judging them or trying to figure it out. I just couldn't stop. I continued to be a witness to this passing storm of emotions. This went on for at least four or five days.

On one of these crying days, I was standing in our private courtyard talking on the phone with Joaquin, who was still in the Philippines. As I looked up I saw Andreas, who appeared out of nowhere, standing perfectly still. I looked at him and started to cry even harder. So I quickly got off the phone and walked over to him.

"You know when the ice caps melt, they turn into rivers that run toward your heart," he said as he stepped even closer to me. "Ice caps are frozen for many, many years before they melt," he added.

With this, I found some way to see these tears as beautiful and transformative. Tears were never natural for me, so maybe I was unfreezing many stuck emotions.

"They are tears of love. Don't attach a story. This is how the Ganges River started," he then offered.

With that, I became reverent to whatever was unfreezing in me and the grace that had come to do the melting.

Later that day, the news hit. Jude, an old devotee of Andreas', was coming to the island on business in several weeks. The history between these two was deep, beginning in Hollywood, where the Buddha Field had begun roughly eighteen years before. The story I was told was that Andreas had helped Jude become a millionaire many years ago by advising him on business. At some point thereafter, Jude left the Buddha Field but remained persistent in finding and seeing Andreas again. But Andreas was very reluctant to have Jude return. Jude was the one who had broken into Andreas' house back in Austin, thrown furniture around his bedroom, threatened him, and was also suspected of sending the accusing e-mail that had thrown the Buddha Field into a tailspin. It was because of Jude that Andreas had fled Austin and had gone into exile, so to speak. Jude had become a self-appointed vigilante. He wanted to come after Andreas for all the wrong he had done. He was considered a class-A threat by Andreas and those close to him because Jude was powerful, influential, and very angry.

He had somehow gotten a threatening message to Andreas that shook everyone up. We felt like Andreas was under a very real threat of physical danger. Satsangs now began to be endless discussions about Jude, the enemy, and Andreas' protection.

CHAPTER 33

Captured

I was talking to Joaquin frequently on the phone. He did not understand why I was crying all the time. The last time he saw me, there was nothing but joy. I would always explain that Andreas worked in strange ways that were not easy to figure out. It seemed as though Joaquin was unable to comprehend the true workings of a mystery school, where logic had no place. I guess you could say that Joaquin was part of the Buddha Field for a short while. He showed up near the end but had spent many years as a seeker and a meditator. It was no accident that he was drawn to the group. However, he didn't have many one-on-one encounters with Andreas.

I was also beginning to wonder what was happening to me.

About this time, Diego, who had been living with Andreas for at least fifteen years, decided to move out. He and his boyfriend Lloyd had rented a house down the street. Whenever someone left, it was always because they were "deluded," according to Andreas—deluded into thinking that there was something or someone or someplace out there that would ultimately satisfy them. So everyone as a group felt sorry for anyone who was falling down that slippery slope.

Diego's exit left a vacant room in Andreas' house, directly above his room. It was a nice room with a view overlooking the ocean, in a very nice house. I'm sure there was a lot of speculation as to who would be moving into the spot formerly reserved for one of his closest disciples. It was a coveted spot indeed.

Andreas let it be known that he wanted me to move in there.

"But I'm here for only one more week," I said. And I thanked him for the offer. The kids were heading back to Texas with Mariela, and I was staying on just for a few days, then I would be returning to Southeast Asia with Joaquin.

"That's OK," he said, possibly thinking that I would never move out.

So very reluctantly, assisted by my children and Mariela, I moved in for the duration of my stay in Hawaii. I felt like a little girl whose parents were dropping me off in a strange boarding school and leaving me there. The children were actually very supportive and encouraging, saying that it was only for a week. I was so sad to see them go. The plan was for me to return to the Philippines after my final week on the island. But this is what I had always asked for—to be close to Andreas and to have the acceptance of my children, even if it was for a short while. Hadn't everything I wished for just come true? Yet somehow I was dreading it instead of looking forward to it, even though the invitation was an honor. I had the feeling that I would never be able to leave. I cleaned the bathroom and the room, which was desperately needed, and bought all new fresh white cotton linens for the bed, also desperately needed. Pante, who slept near Andreas' room downstairs and had no closet or any real space of her own, asked if she could put some clothes in my closet.

"Of course," I told her.

Andreas had a way of keeping disciples around. There were many times when people wanted to leave but were hooked into staying. There were countless flight reservations changed and lots of money lost as people listened to guidance about the timing of a trip or a visit or any kind of travel. He also had a way of keeping you in the Buddha Field by simply saying that you were deluded if you left. He told people they were just chasing desire, which would lead them to "miss" this life. This is why it shocked everyone when I announced I was leaving for a short trip to another island for a few days. I knew, simply by the looks on their faces, that some people were thinking, *How can she do that?* This is one of the reasons that Joaquin thought my relationship with Andreas was different. Unlike other disciples, I could come and go as I pleased.

Joaquin had been telling me for months about his two friends who lived on a neighboring island only thirty minutes away by air.

"You have to go and meet them. That's all there is," he repeated on the phone one night.

One of his friends was a well-known herbalist. When I spoke to him on the phone, he seemed like a long-lost brother I had never met. We planned to work with flower remedies when I came to see him. Joaquin's other friend lived at a high altitude near the mouth of a volcanic crater.

It was very early in the morning on the day of my flight, and I was packing. As I turned around there was Andreas, totally still, standing at the sliding glass door to my room. He always had this way of just appearing. Without a word, he walked in. I was not used to him being in my room, as he never really went in anyone's room but his own. It felt very private. He spoke to me about staying in the shakti breath on my trip and he gave me shakti. He told me to be his hands out there and suggested I get in contact with Phil, one his older disciples who was no longer with him. They had a falling out, of which I never knew the details. Andreas wanted me to see him. I know that the two of them had been in contact recently after a period of no contact.

"OK, sure, I will see him," I answered, although I really didn't want to have any obligations. This was my trip, and I wasn't planning on doing service the whole time. While I was devoted to Andreas, I was still very independent. And while I appreciated and received wisdom from him, I felt ruled by him. I felt obligated to Andreas, and yet I resented him at the same time.

The trip was gorgeous, and Joaquin was right about his two friends. We had a beautiful connection. The herbalist lived in an outdoor paradise. His kitchen was fashioned out of the side of a small hill. He had an outdoor shower and slept in a geodesic dome large enough for a bed and some small furniture. His neighbors were Osho devotees who had a Balinese temple built for the sole purpose of meditation and Tango. I took a nap in this temple and decided that this exact altitude and climate was the perfect and most appealing for my body. This is also probably why this area is such a desirable place to live.

His other friend lived near the mouth of a volcanic crater in the vortex of some very powerful mother-earth energy. We hiked near his home and came across the *stupa* that had been built for a certain *rinpoche* several years ago and was also dedicated to the Dalai Lama, who had made an appearance. This rinpoche, having every intention of returning someday, had blessed the temple and surrounding grounds,. There were prayer flags that flapped in the crystal clear air of a very loud silence. It felt like a Tibetan temple in Nepal and had a very familiar feeling to me. It was run by an American monk who lived there. He kept a vigil of burning incense and lit fires as if the master would return at any moment. He was completely devoted, month after month and year after year. When I met him, it was like walking up to an exotic and sacred animal that had not seen people in quite a while. His hut was very simple, with lots of native berries and nuts in bowls. He offered us water, which we took. I wished I had an offering for the temple, but I had had no idea I would be encountering this auspicious scene. We went inside and meditated in the energetic and visual splendor of this rich, sacred temple. The presence of the divine was so strong there, I can even now transport myself back and still see the candle flames, no doubt still burning in total love and devotion.

On my way out, I made an attempt to see Phil. He was on a different part of the island in low country, and I was to also check out some rental houses while in the area. This was part of the plan for Andreas' protection: to move him to another island while Jude was in town. All of this took a lot longer than I expected, so I had to stay an extra day. Phil and I finally met up for lunch, and I was so surprised. He was a beaming, ecstatic, joy-filled devotee who was a paraplegic whom Marcus and Maximus had taken care of for nearly a decade.

The light shining through him was so bright it was overwhelming. Tears came to our eyes as we talked about our journeys over the last many years with Andreas. Phil acknowledged that the way to freedom was through serving a master, but the master was now within him. I was still crying, but this time I knew why. I was so completely happy for my brother, who was sitting in the space of liberation. I felt like finally someone had graduated and made it. This filled me with joy beyond words. It had not been for nothing.

After I returned, I was anxious to share with everyone my journey from the healer, to the selfless service and surrender of the Tibetan monk, and to my brother the disciple who had found freedom and unconditional love. This created a big reaction from everyone, because no one else had become enlightened, and who was I to know who was enlightened? It seemed to push everyone's button as to what enlightenment really was and who, in their opinion, would be entering that state. But I saw what I saw and I felt what I felt.

I shared and I cried, cried, and cried. I apologized for my humanness and whatever it was that kept me from my freedom and from truly serving Andreas selflessly. I cried for all the years I had been *trying so hard.* I cried for my brothers and sisters who had given everything in their pursuit of true freedom. But the biggest thing I cried about on this night was that I knew I couldn't do it anymore. I wondered if all my tears from the past two weeks had been from the grief of knowing I would be leaving Andreas, the island, and the Buddha Field. I had to move on. Had I reached the limit of my surrender? Even in my clear moment of deciding to leave, somehow I felt like I was giving up and not totally surrendering.

For the next few days, as I was sneaking off and talking to Joaquin on the phone, I was becoming more and more irritated and frustrated. These two worlds were becoming very polarized: my relationship with Joaquin and my relationship with Andreas. I started to doubt everything. Was my relationship with Joaquin just one big escape, stuck in the second chakra of success, sex, and power? Was I once again giving all my power away just to "get" love from Joaquin and from Andreas?

Andreas and his entourage always went to the gym on Tuesday and Saturday afternoons as a group (of course). However, I was doing my own thing more and more, and I started going to the gym in the mornings. One day, while I fished through my gym bag on the trunk of my car, I found myself standing next to a man fishing through his gym bag on the trunk of his car. He was a very dark and tough-looking Hawaiian covered in tribal tattoos from head to toe, and in very good shape. I asked him if he had another piece of gum, and he said *yes* and offered me one. I quickly found out that he was a professional fighter and in training for an upcoming fight. As we talked more, he invited me to work out with him. "Sure," I replied. I knew I would learn something and definitely get a good workout. So off we went into the gym. He got the VIP treatment at the door, and I was welcomed as his special guest. It was a great workout, and I soon learned he had a very sweet side (nothing is ever as it appears) and was interested in what I was doing in

Hawaii. I gave him a mild version of the spiritual training I was involved in. He seemed very interested. Once again, the bee was drawn to the honey.

His name was Freddy.

CHAPTER 34

The Buddha Field Machine

We began to see flyers around the island of Jude's upcoming speaking engagement. He had become very successful selling nutritional products and was coming to do a seminar. There was more news that he was "coming after Andreas." This veiled threat could mean physical violence, media exposure, or some sort of legal action. This changed everything, because now precautions had to be made. It was time to put a wall of protection around Andreas.

The scene reminded me of all the movies I had seen about the Kennedy family and their famous "Kennedy Machine," which rose into action when there was a family crisis or scandal. In this case, it was the Buddha Field Machine. Volunteers rose up and offered services that were suggested by Andreas.

Somehow I became the one in charge of finding bodyguards and detectives, as well as going to the police station and finding out about what could be done about this "threat."

"Mata Hari," as Andreas called me a few times, was now in action. I had a new role to play in this culture of "protection." Somehow I was becoming my savior's savior.

This kind of work definitely brought out some interesting characters. We actually met with a professional hit man in a bar. Of course, we didn't hire him. I was surprised to find that these types of services were so readily available and inexpensive. Those who were offering looked like they would do it for free. It was all very dramatic, secretive, and dark.

One day it dawned on me that Freddy would make a great bodyguard, so I decided to approach him. Of course, he was interested. I arranged a meeting with Andreas and Freddy at the gym. Andreas did a good job of mesmerizing Freddy, which did not surprise me. He later told me that he thought Freddy was "open," which did surprise me. Thus was born a bodyguard disciple.

As the date of Jude's arrival neared, the energy required to coordinate all this was becoming overwhelming. It felt like a secret service operation—securing the building, scheduling and having security in place, tracking and scheduling Andreas' whereabouts, investigating other locations, planning an entire group move for the week Jude was in town, seeking legal counsel for possible scenarios—the list was endless. And I could see that there would be considerable expense. I started growing very weary of all this intense coordination with the looming question of who was going to pay for it. So here I was, spending so much time with this while Joaquin was waiting for me with open arms in Southeast Asia. The scales were finally tipping, and "total selfless service to The Master" was starting to not work for me anymore.

I knew that I wanted out, but was not quite sure how to extricate myself from all this. I remember thinking, *Wow. All these people, doing all this work for free, what a "master at something"!*

"You know, Giselle, I don't know how to tell you this, but you are supposed to be living in your Master's house, who is supposed to be an enlightened being, and you are really just becoming a total bitch. I don't know what is happening or why you are so uptight, but it is really causing problems with us. It feels like you can't even fucking leave there. What is going on?" Joaquin was very frustrated with me over the phone one night.

He was right. I was really anxious and not happy. It was impossible to explain to someone how intense it was there. There is a movie called *V for Vendetta* in which the main character lives for months in a prison cell, only to realize one day that all she had to do was open the door, which had never been locked, and walk out. To me, it is what we do all the time. We become prisoners of our own circumstances, and we do this to ourselves. This is certainly what I had been doing—with the help of a Master.

CHAPTER 35

The Scarlet Cleansing

Before sunrise one morning there was a knock on my door. It was Jason, one of Andreas' attendants.

"Giselle, he wants so see you right away," he whispered through the door. "Just come exactly as you are." I got out of bed in my tank top and boy shorts, barefoot, and walked downstairs to Andreas' room. He was sitting in his chair, and behind him the sky was just barely starting to turn pink as the sun was beginning to rise over the Pacific. His eyes were closed.

There was no greeting, as usual. Not too many hellos or good-byes, only "namaste." I sat down in front of him on the floor, not feeling the least bit self-conscious in my underwear.

People in this house, including him, walked around frequently in hardly any clothes.

"Close your eyes," he said next. For those of us in the Buddha Field, these words were like the invocation. These words announced the start of the exercise in class or of a cleansing session. It meant go into meditation and descend down the steps as in the beginning of a hypnotic exercise.

Since this was not the typical session, formality was thrown to the wind, and he went right into describing a scene. I didn't quite know if it was an exercise or a cleansing session.

"There is a fire, can you see it? There is smoke rising as if you are looking back at ruins. Be there," he began. I took a moment to see if I was there. "It is a long, long time ago. Do you see the temple burning?" he continued.

Obviously he was looking into a past life, and I tried to find myself there. Past-life experiences were not uncommon in cleansing sessions. I spent a couple of minutes trying to see if this world would come into focus, but I felt like I was only using my imagination.

"You are crying. Why are you crying?" he said next. Since I wasn't really there, I had no idea why I was crying.

"I'm not sure," I answered, still trying to relate to this. Maybe it was just too early in the morning.

"You are crying because you didn't save your guru. Don't you see, you had a chance, but you missed in that lifetime? What do you see?" he asked.

"Something red," I said, because I did have a flash of color in my mind's eye. In fact, it was the same familiar deep blood red I had experienced in dreams.

"You are seeing the color of my robe at that time. Now here you are again with the same situation in this life," he continued. "You have a chance to save the guru again instead of letting him die like he did last time. Don't you see this is the chance you have been waiting for?" I didn't answer. I was not seeing any of that. But I was feeling like a trap was being set so I would stay forever and save the guru. He knew my psychology well, and he knew this was a big button for me. He knew about David, my boyfriend who had committed suicide, and how in my mind, if you don't save someone, they die.

The rest of the session was a blur as my mind was trying to wrap around what I had just heard. I assumed he was talking about his situation with the drama of Jude coming to town and my role in saving or protecting him from harm.

As I walked back up to my room, I dared to let myself think about what had just happened. I felt like he was leading me and suggesting that I was having that experience. However, the blood red velvet robe felt so familiar. Was it true? Was I having another chance to protect the guru in this lifetime, or was he just planting fear in me so I wouldn't leave? Was my mind playing a trick on me to avoid surrendering?

I decided to plan my exit.

I didn't tell anyone about this experience for quite a while. I just let it soak in. I got on the computer and started looking for flights as soon as possible. I called my friend Margarite and jokingly asked her if she would drive the getaway car to the airport when I made my escape. She laughed and then said, "Sure," in a way that I knew she understood and would do it.

She would have to pick me up at four in the morning. I would pack my bags and leave them outside so when she came, I could just slide out the door without creating too much noise. This would be difficult because you could hear everything with all the windows open and no air conditioning running. That was my plan.

But earlier in the evening, while Andreas was having bodywork, I decided to tell him after all. I sent a message to him letting him know I was leaving. After he was done, he called me into his room. He was still lying on his back on the massage table. I know he wasn't happy about me leaving. He became incredibly sweet and loving, as if his girlfriend were going away. He wanted me to give him a kiss on his forehead, and he held my hand. This affection was very unusual. It was really hard to detach myself from this situation physically, spiritually, emotionally, and mentally.

My spiritual path had turned into "survival while serving," as I was no longer coming from a place of devotion but of simply wanting to escape. The words "total surrender equals total freedom" kept ringing in my ears. Was this my test for total surrender? Is this why the road was narrow and few survived? Well then, I was not going to make it.

But I did make my flight to Southeast Asia early that morning.

CHAPTER 36

The Truth About Saviors

On the eight-hour plane ride, I immediately started to get some perspective, now that I was not in the fire. I wrote a letter to my brothers and sisters:

To my fellow disciples,

I am on the plane, between physical worlds, so to speak. The gap in the air between two physical realities. As I leave the island and the "space" I have been in physically, I feel the move into the density of maya. It is as if I have been watching a movie with the sound off and now the volume is slowly being turned up. The senses of the body start to sharpen, and slow motion now moves into real time. Maya is dialing in. How can we explain to others the otherworldly dimension of the Buddha Field and its energetic field?

As I see all of you, still sleeping in your beds, it is with immense love and reverence that I bow to you all. Not for anything other than what you have chosen in this life. I'm not talking about your current situation, but the choice to relentlessly pursue truth. I am moved to tears at this simple yet profound fact, and touched to the core. There are no words to express the awe of someone devoting his life to truth on the scale at which you offer this. Every encounter and every experience ultimately shows me the most compassionate and generous love I am capable of accepting. I too continue to devote my life to the same, but not under the same circumstances, because I have realized one thing:

There is no savior on the planet other than truth.

Love, Giselle

At this point, it was time to really take a look at all the rumors that had been circulating about Andreas. There were rumors that several men in the group had accused Andreas of sexual misconduct. According to the rumors, these men were asked to expose themselves and sometimes pleasure themselves during a cleansing session. I can see these different men sitting there, at their most vulnerable moment, speaking with the one in whom they have put all their trust, and then they are told to surrender. They are told that the way to enlightenment is through surrender to The Master. They had given up their lives as they knew them to find true freedom. Their hearts and souls were fully open to this being. He asked them to trust him as he guided them to drop their minds and go beyond. And so many would, only to feel violated, manipulated, ashamed, confused and broken. Even today, many of them are still struggling with the emotional scars of this abuse.

There are countless stories involving sexual and emotional abuse within the Buddha Field. There was actual sex with quite a few male disciples, both straight and gay, that went on for years. There is one story about one of Andreas' long-term live-in boyfriends who, after falling in love and having sex with an HIV-positive partner, was told to get down on his knees and give The Master a blow job. There was the story of another long-term boyfriend who was really in love with Andreas when he caught him in bed with another disciple. Andreas denied that this happened and that his boyfriend "did not see that." Upon this insane denial, the boyfriend returned to a crack addict's life. Andreas then assigned two female devotees to live with the addict and take care of him. When the girls confessed they couldn't do it anymore because they were afraid he was going to die, Andreas just gave instructions on whom to call first if he did OD. According to some, his sexual appetite was voracious, and during many cleansing sessions he was watching pornography, with the sound muted, on the television positioned behind the disciple's head. At first it really surprised me how many straight guys said yes to Andreas' advances. But when I remembered my own surrender to this master, it didn't surprise me at all.

It was easy for me to turn a blind eye when I first heard the rumors. I was good at being quiet. I was rewarded for being quiet. I had been the confidante to others because I never betrayed a confidence.

After all, they were just rumors. I refused to read the e-mail that went out, accusing him of being a fugitive, having a false identity, being a sexual predator, a liar, and a manipulator. Besides, this had not been *my* experience.

I didn't want it to be over. I loved my life. I loved the search for enlightenment. However, after a while, I could no longer turn a blind eye.

The death of the Buddha Field as we knew it was imminent, at least for me and most of the others. The experience of this death was no different than the death of someone very close to you. I would have to endure the five stages of grief: denial, anger, bargaining, depression, and acceptance. I just happened to hang out in the denial stage for way too long.

I felt ashamed for having someone so close to me, a family member, being accused of being a criminal or a fake. A guru is more than a family member. He plays the role of father, mother, brother, friend, sweetheart—whatever is needed for your awakening. This adult connection was by far the deepest in my life.

Was it up to us to take complete responsibility for our experience? What is the difference between surrender and completely giving up control of your life?

I read a book by Nityananada, Muktananda's guru, which said that the fastest way to liberation was to do service directly for the guru. However, it was not recommended much because it always hit a nerve and caused controversy. Surrender has many definitions.

CHAPTER 37

The Truth About Heroes

Six months later, I was working out with Maximus in his gym on a cold and rainy day.

"I just keep having this thought, Giselle. Do you still have those trust papers you signed when you bought the house for Andreas?" Maximus asked out of the clear blue. Even though Maximus was never supposed to know that I bought the house, I had confessed the truth to him as my discipleship was melting down, several months earlier. He didn't even bat an eye upon hearing it.

"Yeah, actually, they are in a bag in the kitchen drawer," I responded. "Why do you ask?" I wanted to know because the subject was hitting a nerve.

"Well, I just have this feeling you should take those papers to a lawyer and have them checked out. I want to start unraveling this mess. Maybe there is a chance that you still have some ownership, and just maybe I can help you sell it and we can do the right thing here," he went on.

"I'll do it."

I went home, called a friend for a good real-estate lawyer, and got a recommendation for a guy named Walter. I called and got an appointment. On the day of our meeting, I drove to a humble little house on the north side of town. I walked in and met Walter in his home office. A tall white-haired man in his sixties with a spectacularly kind face greeted me. Our eyes met and we said nothing for a full minute. Open-eye meditation was not exactly what I was expecting. He motioned me to sit down.

"How can I help you?" he asked sincerely.

I paused, wondering how in the world to begin to explain this situation. He knew nothing about me, only that I needed real-estate trust advice. I took a chance because of the compassion and intelligence in his eyes. I told him everything.

"I bought a house for my spiritual master and he had me put it in a blind trust, under his control, at the time I purchased it. Now I want to see if I can somehow sell it and get my money back. Can you tell me who exactly owns this house by looking at all these documents?" I asked.

Without missing a beat, he looked at me and said, "Are you ready to leave your spiritual master for good?"

This caught me by surprise. The weight of his question and his tone in its all-embracing loving-kindness brought a tear to my eye. I hesitated, thought, and then clearly said, "Yes."

"Well, alright then, give me about twenty minutes to read all these documents." As he slowly spread out all the papers, he told me this story: "You know, Giselle, I am an ex-disciple of Muktananda, who was plagued with sexual scandal. I got out before all the drama happened because I knew that I had already received the greatest gift I could ever receive. I knew I had it in me and didn't need to stick around for the fireworks."

After breathing in this amazing serendipity, and after about ten more minutes, he looked up and said, "Well, guess who owns the house."

"Who?"

"You do, Giselle. Now go and sell it, and do whatever you want with the money," he said.

And so I did. Maximus listed it, and he sold it for me. I paid myself back, and I paid Maximus back for the car he bought Andreas.

This wasn't the first time a spiritual leader had been plagued by scandal. Were any of them really enlightened? It was hard to watch my own master sliding down that slippery slope.

Then all the stories began to circulate from many different disciples about what had happened to them over the years. Many felt betrayed, lied to, manipulated, abused, and treated unfairly. I could fill books with each individual's story. Many have sought therapy to heal the wounds. Some have begun to take medication, as they cannot seem to get their lives back on track. For some, they came to Andreas in their late teens and spent most of their adult lives with him. This was all they knew.

Then a blog came out called *After the Truth* written by an ex-disciple, which was a very intelligent recounting of people's genuine experiences with Andreas. This began the healing for the group. For me, I felt like it was a detoxification from those aspects of Andreas that were not from higher consciousness, but were from an unchecked ego. It seems that somewhere along the way he went from seeing himself as the one who leads the way to the one who *is* the way.

I have noticed that everyone who was involved in the Buddha Field had a completely different experience. I see many who are now focusing on the messy ending, like a really bad divorce. I have chosen to focus on the juicy middle part, where the teachings felt pure, love was shared, where we were waking from our sleep and life was more uncomfortable than ever. There is no enlightenment without undoing the ego. And our egos did deconstruct to some degree by our experiences with Andreas.

My relationship with Andreas was complex. Like a child, I had developed an unconditional love for him which made it possible for me to overlook the evil aspects of his mission: to control, to separate us from others, and to pose as a spiritual authority who made us question our own instincts as human beings with emotions and a complex array of experiences. In our quest to transcend, we descended into an inauthentic life of the mind and ego disguised as achieving a new sense of unity and personal power. We were not having the pure experience of the heart we had all hoped for. We could not trust ourselves anymore, and our own beautifully individual spiritual paths had been crushed into one another's in a mixture of confusion, betrayal, pain, and longing. He was human, after all. And so were we.

But like divorce or death, even this extraordinary experience played its part in my journey, and I wouldn't change it for anything. I believe we all had unique karma together, and the way one chooses to emerge from a devastating life event is even more important than the event itself. We have a choice. I choose to love my experience in the Buddha Field.

Masters are not meant to be liked. They never compliment you or tell you you're doing great. They never tell you that you have arrived at your destination. A master will never fix up your life and make it better; that is not his role. His role is to wake you up from your life. This is not a minor thing—this is everything.

This is why I am grateful.

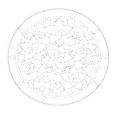

CHAPTER 38

Am I Enlightened Now?

The short answer is "no." But I believe that this dance I've begun has opened powerful doors to moments of enlightenment and has changed the way I see life and live it. Spiritual maturity is a lifelong journey full of expansions and contractions.

Why are people drawn to awakened beings, or beings we perceive to be more awakened than ourselves, even corrupt beings that we believe to be awakened? Why and how do these beings magnetize others toward them? Because we believe they are clear vessels, not layered with filters, totally available to us, to feel us and hear us in ways that we may not be used to. They are free to fully tune in to us. They are free to experience exactly what is happening in the moment. There is nothing in the way, and that is intoxicating.

I believe that currently there are many fully awakened beings bubbling up around the globe, with many more to follow in a very short time. Just as a bubble rises, it expands until it explodes and dissolves into all there is, only to be followed by more bubbles of pure consciousness rising.

I have been feeling free these days. If you told me that I would have traveled the world with a treasure hunter, began selling vintage cars and started writing books and poetry, I wouldn't have believed you. My life now seems to be about creating, experiencing, and playing. In fact, my motto is sometimes "I don't know what I might do!" And that's the fun part.

And then if you told me that this was nothing compared to my inner adventure, I still wouldn't have believed you.

I had always imagined my spiritual journey would take me to a place where I was no longer interested in any worldly pursuits, such as romance, sex, sensual delights, travel, beautiful things, or anything material. Even in the Buddha Field all these things existed. I also thought I would be in a place where I no longer had a bad day, or felt petty, irritated, or impatient. I thought I would be beyond all the emotional messiness of being human. But as I begin to feel liberated from my own limiting mind, I realize that this path of love is not about being free *from* humanness but being free *to be* completely human. The ups and downs are there, but no matter what is happening on the outside, my inner experience is starting to remain untouched. I am seeing in more and more people the "LOOK" of being in love that I have so desperately craved. This is happening with much more frequency and the love that has fueled the drive for people to wake up is now the love that is fueling the Ascension.

I AM MY OWN GURU.

EPILOGUE

Since my experience in the Buddha Field, I occasionally intersect with former members around the country. Slowly and with great care and compassion, they have begun to piece their lives back together and rebuild long lost relationships.

Then one day, I received a phone call from a disciple, someone who had been close to me in the Buddha Field. He confessed to me that he had been a sexual slave to Andreas for many years. He was trying to find ways to heal from his experience when he suddenly learned that the reign of Andreas' manipulative spiritual court was not yet over. Through reliable sources this former disciple discovered that Andreas had a new flock. He was fully operational in Hawaii and indoctrinating a new crop of spiritual seekers.

I was shocked. How could Andreas still be mesmerizing and influencing people on this level? He had seventy-five new devotees who were reaching, searching and would probably do anything for him. Like many of us in the original Buddha Field, enough was enough. Over the next few years, our stories will come to light. Hopefully, through sharing our personal trials, we will warn the open hearted to avoid and distrust Andreas as a leader and as a man. Certainly, he deserves consequences for his crimes against the men he abused. And the universe will take care of the crimes he committed against the hearts of the seekers and those on the courageous and tender path of waking up.

Made in the USA
San Bernardino, CA
08 November 2012